# TICKET TO FREEDOM

# TICKET TO FREEDOM

H. J. Spiller, DFM

WILLIAM KIMBER

First published in 1988

British Library Cataloguing in Publication Data

Spiller, H.J.
   Ticket to freedom.
   1. France. Great Britain, Royal Air Force.
   Personal. Escapes, 1939–1945. Biographies
   I. Title
   940.54'4941'0924

ISBN 1-85260-200-7

William Kimber & Co Ltd is part of the
Thorsons Publishing Group, Wellingborough,
Northamptonshire, NN8 2RQ, England.


Printed and bound in Great Britain by
Redwood Burn Limited, Trowbridge, Wiltshire


1  3  5  7  9  10  8  6  4  2

This book is written as a memorial to the following who died for freedom:

Squadron Leader Sidney Horace Fox, DFM
Flight Sergeant Norman Alexander Mercer
Sergeant Philip Charles Heath
Sergeant Lawrence Fitzsimmons
Sergeant Henry Frederick Wood

Antoine Renaud
Edouard Verpraet
Aimable Fouquerel
Francia Usandizanga

. . . and all the others who helped me without counting the cost.

*Ami, si tu tombes*
*Un ami sort de l'ombre*
*Te remplacer*

(from the *Chant des Partisans*)

# Contents

# List of Illustrations

# Acknowledgements

Apart from the great debt which I owe to all the people within these pages who assisted my return, I should like to acknowledge the following who helped to get the book written: my wife Betty for her continual encouragement, my daughter Laura whose idea it was that the story should be told, my son Tim who read and corrected the written manuscript whilst giving me valuable feedback as a younger reader, and Jo Clark for her ideas on the structure of the story and her patience in typing the final manuscript. My thanks are also due to Christopher Ailsby, Norman Franks and Alan Cooper for the loan of photographs.

H.J.S.

CHAPTER ONE

# Up

I woke up with my nose pressed against the wooden wall of the aircrew dispersal hut. There was an ache somewhere behind my eyes and a tell tale bitter taste in my mouth. The saloon bar of The Dying Gladiator in Brigg had certainly been jumping last night. Some party! Not the best time to have one in a busy Ops week, but things had been getting more dicey with a lot of the senior crews getting the chop. The skipper wouldn't like it, he didn't go much on pre-ops boozing, although he half accepted the tendency of crews to release their tensions that way. My head told me that he might be right. I painfully lowered myself out of bed and shuffled towards the crude window to check the weather. Lincolnshire was wearing a gown of fine mist.

God, was it that time? 9.15 a.m. and breakfast 'up the swanee' for a start. In the October half-light I peered across the room at the humped figure in the opposite bed. Chalky was still flaked out and ought to have been after flying for two out of the last three nights. Probably didn't get in until 4 a.m. from last night's effort against Düsseldorf. I mused absent-mindedly, rocking to and fro in my bare feet, on my luck at having stood down for the last fortnight. One of the perks of being in the flight commander's crew, I suppose, or if you looked at it another way one of the disadvantages because your tour of ops was over an extended period, but at least you lived longer. Next time we went three of us would finish our second tours with fifty up each; old hands who were considered to be lucky to fly with. If you got that far 'Nebby' or the Good Lord or whatever you called him must be on your side. Experience helped, of course, but there was no flak shell that couldn't blow up the best. The nightly lottery in the barrages high over the Happy Valley of the Ruhr, and elsewhere, proved that. Mentally I gave myself a 'kick up the trousers', my inner voice telling me to move down some other line of thought; maybe a cold shower would help.

The ablutions hut wasn't as empty as I had reckoned. Jock and Phil and a few others were shaving and generally washing away the ravages of another thrash in Scunthorpe – The Oswald more than likely; the Sods Opera cabaret there was popular with the troops. Choruses of 'You look rough!' and 'Not time for the annual shower, is it?' vibrated on my sensitive ears as I shambled towards the shower area. Later I would singe their ears but survival was the priority now and I needed that shower to feel alive. As the healing waters poured out of the battered shower head I dreamily reflected on the lads outside.

Jock, a laconic Scot from Aberdeen, swarthy, slim, and energetic, and Phil, a genial London lad from Putney, nearly six feet, heavier built and slow moving, were both gunners in our present crew, tail and mid-upper in that order, highly efficient and keen and happy to be with us. With luck they wouldn't have much trouble finishing their first tour after Sid, Woolly and I had stepped down. Some crews came from Operational Training Units together and lived and shared their off duty hours as a family, but we had been assembled from various backgrounds and were individuals within a team. Strange that we shared the same enclosed airspace in our Halifax and experienced together the same mouth-drying death dance over a growing number of burning towns and yet each had his own private life, personal friends and pursuits when we were not flying. I really didn't know them at all well, but I knew one thing for sure: that up there, they would be protecting me at all times, if necessary placing their own lives at risk. The bond between us was a professional one but it had that element of light-heartedness that covered any inner anxiety that might come over to the others as fear or panic. If courage had any definition at all, that was it. It was the professional determination to do the job for which you were trained despite whatever difficulties arose. Sid and I had already been given gongs after our first tours for just that; no conspicuous gallantry, just dogged determination and the will to go on.

I turned off the shower as someone hammered on the door of the cubicle and shouted.

'Dizzy?'

It was Mac, a B flight wireless operator and bosom drinking chum.

'Yeah?' I gurgled still with a mouthful of water.

'You're wanted in the flight commander's office right away!'

'OK, Mac.'

Time for a shave yet, even if the balloon has gone up. Seems to be a lot of engine noise out at dispersal, maybe we go tonight.

Looking at myself in the shaving mirror I saw a chubby pink face, dark brown wavy hair, couldn't be more than eighteen, a straggle of hairs on the upper lip and two front teeth missing, long since taken out by an RAF dentist. I had contracted frost-bite in the upper front gum after flying in a Fairey Battle with the rear hood open trying to see how long I could go without an oxygen mask at 22,000 feet. My career as an air observer had nearly come to grief on that, but for an understanding commanding officer. I shook my head at my reflection and quickly cleaned the teeth I had left and strode out of the ablutions hut feeling much better.

On the way to the hangar with the camp roads bustling with airmen and airwomen moving in all directions, I had the feeling that Elsham Wolds had a separate life in which the flyers took no part other than as temporary interlopers with an existence limited by their luck in the air war. Their life was so unnatural, changing within hours from the safe comfort of the mess bars and chairs to the ever nearness of death in the concentrated barrages on target approaches, topped only by the sheer terror of being coned by searchlights and attacked by a night fighter. And then back again to the peace and comfort they had known, if they were lucky, to await another round of aerial roulette. Even the phrase 'Survival of the fittest' didn't apply. You lived for the day, or maybe a day, but the camp went on. I finished soliloquizing and reached the hangar. Most of the effects of the previous night had gone and I felt that the skipper could be faced with a fair chance of my escaping a reprimand.

'So you managed it at last!' Sid was in curt form as I appeared in the doorway.

'Sorry, sir. Overslept, I'm afraid.' I really didn't sound convincing.

'Because of what, is more important,' Sid countered. 'You had better be sober, we're flying tonight.'

'I'm as bright as a button, sir. Had a fairly quiet night for me!'

Sid narrowed his eyes and smiled. I'm off the hook then.

'Navigator's briefing is at 1300. I'll look in shortly afterwards.'

'OK, sir,' I said crisply and gave him a smart salute, totally out of character but decidedly out of relief.

We had done twelve ops together now with 103 Squadron and knew each other's strengths and weaknesses. Looking at him now, dark hair, piercing eyes, mid-height but lithe as a panther, to me he was the epitome of the bomber captain, keen, pugnacious and overtly fearless. A squadron leader now, he had come up from the ranks and was the complete commander. His weakness? Well, he suffered from sinus trouble and hated to fly high, and because of this we were mostly forced to carry out our ops somewhere in the 6,000 to 8,000 feet band with the main force sometimes the same distance above us. It made for an exciting life, but as a crew we never referred to it or made a fuss. We had the best pilot on the station and had utter confidence in his ability. In his own way, I believe he felt the same about us, which probably accounted for the fact that he never considered changing any of the crew. Twice he stood down to let the station commander take us on thousand bomber raids and he once said he was proud that his crew had been chosen, although he would have dearly loved to have gone himself.

The crew room was filled with a number of apprehensive crews excitedly discussing the lists of those picked for the night's operation; the relief in the eyes of some was hardly disguised. For them lay ahead twenty-four hours of more or less guaranteed survival and all the joys that could be packed into the off-duty hours. They usually left after a short while, strangely feeling that they were not part of the small community who would now prepare for the serious business of ensuring that such problems that can befall the sloppy and unwary airman did not have the opportunity to arise. Small groups began to break off to go to dispersal to check their aircraft and to make sure that their equipment was complete and working. The more experienced among them knew that the routine of check and double-check was the thin dividing line between a successful return and the prospect of eternal hallelujahs.

I was digging out my navigation bag from the crew locker as Woolly and Peewee broke through the milling throng.

'We're off to dispersal, Diz. Any gen on the target yet?' called Woolly.

'You should know better than that,' I countered.

Woolly was our wireless operator, recently commissioned after his first tour. Fair curly hair, angular, a Lancastrian without any side, he didn't attempt to stand on rank. He knew radio work backwards and was a treasure to have aboard an aircraft. Peewee, a bomb aimer and front gunner, a broad Scot from Edinburgh, tall and talented not only as an aircrew member but also as an artist in oils. He had done several pictures already of scenes around the camp and in flight. His long jutting chin spilling out of a flying helmet gave you the assurance that here was a determined character and on your side, to boot.

'Oh well. If you haven't anything to tell us we'll see you over at dispersal. Hope it's not the Big City.'

Woolly's voice tailed off as an anxious prayer. You and me both I thought, Berlin is no place to finish off a tour. Perhaps we were both getting edgy, the last hurdle and all that; life was beckoning at the end of a dark tunnel filled with flak and shouting.

Everything seemed to be in order in the navigation bag apart from my stock of pencils that needed sharpening, and I busied myself in the crew room putting new points on them. Navigators over Europe worked through a series of immediate crises as aircraft stumbled their way against a host of distractions avoiding surprise fire and the ever present beams of searchlights. The course of the aircraft changed many times and each time frenzied fresh calculations were necessary. It may seem inconsequential but sharpened pencils were a life-line to me and I placed them here and there around the navigator's table so that at least one would be available in a flap.

Satisfied, I wandered out of the hangar to catch a transport to dispersal where I found Woolly and Peewee engrossed in their routine checks. Jock and Phil had been there some time and so had Fitz, our flight engineer. On him rested the operational efficiency of the aircraft and the sight of his short and slight frame topped with frizzy hair bent over the instrument panels in deep concentration, always gave me an almost divine assurance that we would be OK. I struggled through the front hatch past him to my own 'office' and went through my own checks, not forgetting to place my pencils, apart from those I would need for the briefing.

With our checks done and wolfing through teas and 'wads' at the mobile Naafi wagon, we ruminated on the various factors which would comprise our evening's entertainment, target, bomb load, weather and aircraft numbers, but we had no real idea as yet. Individually ruminating, we returned to the hangar in an unconsciously agreed silence; the visit to the aircraft and the preparations going on had begun to have an effect on nerves, however subtle, and until we had returned from wherever it was any humour would be forced and any conversation would be half-hearted unless it related to the job in hand.

On an impulse I checked the parachute list and found that my own was two days overdue for re-packing. It was just as well that I had seen it, although it wasn't really a hazard. In any case it gave me a chance to chat up Brenda, the WAAF packer, whose charms were not for all and sundry, and you were made aware of it if you tried it on a little too cheekily.

Facing her across the enormously long parachute packing table I tried a 'How about coming to Brigg or Scunthorpe with me if I get back from the gates of Hell?'

Her smile was a little too sweet. 'The only pulling you'll do is on that rip ring on the chute.'

She meant it, so I complied with a sigh. As if by magic out blossomed yards and yards of pure white silk; what a wonderful art it was to get it all back in a parachute pack.

'On your way. It'll be ready at three.' Her tone was imperious and final. Disappointed, I slouched towards the door of the hut only to catch her voice saying, 'Dizzy.' I turned questioningly. 'Be careful,' she added.

Her eyes and voice were tender. She had seen a good many go, including her husband, and knew what the risks were. She and her like, all the ground-staff who worked sometimes at all hours so that we could take the hero's part and strut about when all went well, were the salt of the earth, and any flier who did not recognise that was not worthy of the name.

Hunger was getting the better of me now and I turned towards the mess hoping to get into the first sitting for lunch. Usually pre-operational inner tensions reduced the natural desire to eat, but I had had nothing much for a whole day apart from the 'wad' at dispersal, and I felt the need. Through the mess door I could see Jock and Peewee, the two flight sergeants, and Phil and Fitz, the sergeants, propping up the bar. As I approached, Jock was already buying a pint shandy for me to match the others on the counter. This was the traditional glass we took together on these occasions and all that we would allow ourselves, bearing in mind the skipper's aversion. Not all crews did the same, some brazened it out and had a few drinks and a few went to their own quarters for a private tipple. The old hands knew better; a clear head kept the balance in your favour.

'We missed the first sitting,' purred Jock. 'I'm no hungry anyhow.' The Aberdeen lilt was strong in his voice. We moved away from the bar and flopped in the handiest armchairs. Apart from a desultory dart game the mess was virtually empty.

'Just like a morgue,' Phil was making a rare observation. 'Typical ops day, not a happy soul in sight,' he finished.

'Roll on briefing,' added Fitz. 'These hours before take-off are pure murder.'

'So are the ones afterwards,' Peewee croaked. 'I could do with some leave.'

Our reverie over the shandies were broken as the mess began to fill up again with satisfied eaters and the bar became noisy with false laughter. We looked at each other and shrugged and moved off to the dining room.

Lunch over, I returned to the hangar to pick up my navigation bag and was one of the first to enter the briefing room. The target information was still covered up but the board was set up longways instead of sideways; well well, we've got a target to the south then, could be Stuttgart or Munich I suppose. Looks a long 'un. Jostling started for the best position as more and more navigators crowded in. The operations officer and the weather man were already busy with their portfolios and charts when the Wing Commander entered. His tall figure and long dark countenance and chin reminded you of Basil Rathbone, and his dark piercing eyes broadcast to all and sundry that here was a man born to authority who would expect 100 per cent effort and get it! Yet he was disliked by a number of crews who would, however, gladly have flown into oblivion behind him because they respected his skill and judgment. As an operational pilot he came close behind Sid.

A brief nod from him and the operations officer took off the wraps from the board. A chorus of whistles went up as the eager eyes around the room saw the red cord of the target route snaking down towards Italy. The final destination was still unknown as the cord hung limply across the Alps, purely as a security measure, so that no unauthorised person could discover the target. Very cunning. A further nod and the operations officer faced the assembly.

'The target for tonight is Milan,' he calmly said, moving to the map and placing his yellow board pin on the centre of the city, then winding on his red cord to complete the route. 'The route chosen is Base – Dungeness – Le Tréport – 4556N/0830E–4544N/0835E – Target, returning direct to Le Tréport and landing at Tangmere.' A low murmur of voices was cut short by the Wing Commander. 'Main briefing is at 1445, when you will be informed of bomb loads, fuel loads, and any gen about ancillary operations to divert the enemy. Now for the weather.'

The met man rose almost apologetically. 'A bit like the curate's egg tonight. There will be a great deal of cloud on the outward journey and you will need to fly through a fairly huge front over mid-France. From there, things get a lot brighter and you should find no cloud over the Alps and very little in the target area. I have prepared the provisional wind forecasts etcetera so that you can get ahead with the flight plans and you will have a further up-date at main briefing.'

Papers began to filter down as he was speaking and I could see why we were finishing at Tangmere. There was a distinct prospect of head winds on the way back and petrol would be at a premium. The south coast aerodrome would be a welcome sight.

'That's all, chaps,' rang out the Wing Commander's voice.

I could hardly contain myself. What a way to finish a tour. A lovely doddle over the centre of France, the Alps in moonlight, an easy Eyetie target and a warm bed at Tangmere with the additional perk of a fighter command mess. Sid tapped me on the shoulder, breaking my train of thought.

'Get on with it, you've only got an hour.' He had been busy in the flight commander's office and had just dashed over to check the route.

'OK, sir. What do you think of it?' I asked.

'Could be worse. See you at the main briefing,' was all I could get out of him. The charts were now being handed out and I settled down to my calculations. The new boys used Dalton computers for their navigational work, as did most of the others and I looked a little like Noah with my old-fashioned course and speed calculator. Be that as it may, I was always there amongst the quickest finishers. With my old instrument I could have a new course calculation in a fraction of a second, a vital factor over enemy territory. By the look of it the trip would last somewhere in the region of 8½ hours, long enough in rough weather. Calculations over, I left my bag in the careful keeping of the operations officer and wandered off to my room for a half hour siesta which I knew would not really lead to sleep. Fortunately I avoided seeing any of the crew so I wasn't subjected to their curiosity as to the night's destination.

Lying prone on my bed was as much as I was going to get in the way of rest, my mind was turning over with all the possibilities that could happen both during and after the flight. Fatal really, because nothing ever happened the way you envisaged it. Perhaps I'll do another stint as an instructor or try to get on the Atlantic Ferry. A film at the camp theatre had sparked off this idea, a sugar-coated American view of the life of crews ferrying Lease Lend aircraft over the Atlantic; the unreality of it appealed to our death-sensitive sense of humour. Ah well, let's get back first. My wrist chronometer told me I had about a quarter of an hour before briefing and I moved up to the mess kitchen to get a cup of tea, one of the perks of being a warrant officer. I milked that dodge quite a bit, helped by the fact that the middle-aged WAAF cook had a soft spot for me. The hot bitter brew chased away the remnants of last night's after effects. I left the empty cup and saucer on top of the hot plate, hugged her shoulder and wandered up to the briefing room.

Already the rows of seats were filling up with an excited gabbling throng, talking mostly about any other thing than the matter in hand. Peewee and Jock had saved a seat between them and looked expectantly as I sat down.

'Well then,' came a gruff Scottish whisper, 'what is to to be the nicht?'

I smiled and said, 'Wait and see. It's a doddle.'

Peewee looked strained. 'Oh my God, it must be Hamburg, the way the wee man is smiling.'

Jock flashed a sympathetic glance across me and added, 'Well, we've no been there very much.'

Sid and Woolly slipped into their seats straight from the officers' mess and nodded their hallos, and quickly behind them came the Group Captain and the Wingco. An immediate hush exemplified the unconscious discipline under which we lived, a curious thing really as aircrews were notoriously high spirited, extrovert and devil may care, yet under certain circumstances both on the ground and in the air they reacted to discipline immediately without thinking. Much of it had to do with the need for such control to enable you to stay alive in tight corners, and there had been some heroic examples of that in the war so far, not to mention our illustrious forerunners in World War I.

The Wing Commander broke the silence from the small rostrum on which the senior officers sat.

'Gentlemen. The target for tonight.' A nod to the operations officer who peeled back the covering from the target board. 'Milan.'

The initial inrush of breath from a hundred mouths quickly turned into delighted chuckles and chit chat. Immediate quiet again as the Wingco held up a restraining hand.

'We are sending eleven aircraft on our longest mission to date which involves a flight over the Alps in moonlight and a round trip of some eight hours. I've no doubt you will find it interesting but don't write this trip off as a milk run. You have some difficult French territory to fly over in terms of vulnerability to night fighters and you may find the Italians a little more aggressive than their colleagues in North Africa. In view of the length of the journey you will be taking second pilots and these will be allocated by the flight commanders. Take-off is at 18.30 and you should be at the target at 22.30. The operations officer and technical officers will now brief you in detail as to target material, fuel and bomb loads and of course the weather man will give you the latest run down on what to expect en route. You have your first chance to take the offensive to the other half of the Axis. Do it well and good luck.'

The rest of the briefing lost none of its interest as each speaker explained in fine detail what was expected of us and what we would be supplied with to carry out effectively the orders of Bomber Command Headquarters, perhaps the personal orders of 'Butch' Harris himself. An air of grimness was now beginning to pervade the assembly and the serious work of absorbing the information supplied was eroding the inner joy that the first news of the target had evoked in each mind. This was going to be some trip! It looked a piece of cake, but no chances please!

As the last of the confidential documents and information was being handed out, the Group Captain rose from his chair, sporting the DSO he had received after the thousand bomber raids he had made with us. His stock was very high with the aircrews, an old man by their standards, but he had been a rugger international and a pilot of some distinction in the peace-time Air Force. In their eyes he had earned his laurels and they were quite happy to serve under him.

'Gentlemen, tonight's effort has a great deal of significance to your squadron. Not only is it the first time that you will have flown over Italian soil but also, that this will be the last operation using the Halifax. Some of you, I know have already become endeared to the aircraft but higher powers than ourselves have decided that every effort must be made to increase the attacking capacity of the Command and the changeover to the Lancaster is therefore inevitable. Sufficient aircraft will be arriving in the next day or two for the station to remain operational without much loss of time. In a way you are at a turning point in history. Put your especial seal on this trip. Good luck.'

With that, the senior officers left the briefing room, whilst the general excitement again burst out of a hundred mouths. The hubbub remained for several minutes until the flight commanders managed to restore order and to inform everyone that the pre-flight meal would be at 16.30 with a final briefing at 17.30 when any deviations from the main briefing would be passed on. We bustled from our chairs throwing off asides and jokes to others around us.

The gunners shot off to make a second check that their heated suits were operating fully. I think that the prospect of the temperature over the Alps was the main factor. Fitz made another visit to dispersal to watch how the maintenance of the aircraft was going, I repaired to the mess picking up my parachute on the way and Sid and Woolly returned to the flight office to tie up the odds and ends which fall to a flight commander. The next few hours, the waiting, would be the worst although it would be hard to detect on the faces of the more battle-hardened crews.

Hardly anyone but the odd navigator was in the mess. Those not flying were no doubt busy with one or other of the emergency drills, practice shooting, simulated bombing runs (using a room fitted with the latest mechanical devices to produce a reasonably life-like representation of flying over enemy territory), or non-flying duties which were designed to hone up one's skills and reflexes. Groundstaff were without doubt hard at it, as they always were, whether we were flying or not, and the remainder of the crews were filling up the time before take-off in their own particular way, some even in prayer.

One of the male cooks was passing time on the snooker table and I joined him for a game, neither of us concentrating and almost content to play it out in desultory fashion. He left after a while to help prepare the pre-flight meal, obviously dying to ask where we were heading for that night but prudent enough to know when to keep silent. The snooker table had lost what interest I had in it and I was glad that I had only leafed through one picture magazine before the lads came in. Maybe it was getting to me too, and I was supposed to be the intrepid one. We placed our chairs in a circle and smoked and chatted away the moments, not really listening to each other but just gaining strength from our communal relationship and sensing the importance of oneness in the next few hours. The meal was a complete contrast, the die was cast, we were mentally prepared for all that might lie ahead and all nervousness appeared to have vanished. We ate ravenously quite differently from the earlier meal when we had no idea of the target, and jokes came thick and fast. The next half hour we would spend in our own quarters, either on our backs, or writing a 'last' letter, or meditating on the odds of seeing tomorrow.

The time soon passed and I began to dress for the evening's entertainment, not forgetting my thick silk vest and 'long johns' which would be indispensable for this trip. A quick check of my good luck charms, a WAAF scarf and a cap badge of the French Tank Corps given to me by a *poilu* during the Battle of France in 1940, and I was ready but not before I had looked in all pockets for any items which would betray my British origin if I happened to be captured. Satisfied, I moved off to round up the lads and we made the pilgrimage in silence up to the flight hangar, except Peewee who was humming a lesser known Scottish air. It helped.

All the crews gathered in the crew room to hear that no changes had been made to any of the briefing material apart from a slight increase to the petrol load which was always handy. Sid allocated the second pilots to each crew and this was the first we had heard of ours, a Sergeant Wood who had just arrived on camp. In fact his luggage was still in the guard room to await his return. Jock and Phil raised their eyebrows but Sid knew what he was doing and after all he was the ideal captain to ease a 'sprog' through his first operation.

To make him feel at home we quickly singled him out and introduced ourselves. He was fresh-faced and chunkily built and looked extremely useful, and he was quite happy to have fallen in with such an experienced crew. Maybe he could take the lads over when Sid, Woolly and I had finished. Why not, but they would need to see first how he coped when it got dicey. Sid had sorted him out some flying kit and while he busied himself adjusting it to suit himself, we went to our own lockers to finish togging-up. Quite a number used Irvin Suits, heavy leather and sheepskin, although I still preferred the Sidcot flying suit, really an overall with a number of useful pockets. Across the left breast of mine I sported a pair of wings with a beer glass in the centre instead of the 'RAF' letters, and the motto 'The Flying Pint'. Another lucky charm from the Battle of France days and an ever reminder of our Dawn Patrol life during the early summer of 1940 in French airfields.

All that remained was for the crews to be allocated transport to take them to their dispersal points, Sid gave a short homily and wished everyone good luck and the Wingco popped in to give his final 'blessing'. We staggered out into the darkening outside world clutching our paraphernalia and boarded an open wagon reserved for the flight commander; another perk. You could just make out the fixed smiles atop all the bulky figures in the mêlée around the various kinds of transport, and you were for a brief moment caught up in the melancholy that some of these might never return. A quick jerk of the clutch and you were back to reality, the hubbub receding in exhaust fumes, to be replaced in very quick time by the eerie silence and loneliness of the dispersal point with its huge black shape pointing ever heavenwards. Several of the groundcrew appeared from the gloom to give us a hand with our equipment and to reassure us of the serviceability of 'D for Donald'. We knew them well enough but somehow we never seemed to have the opportunity to show our appreciation apart from an odd glass or two in the mess or the village local. Our working relationship was very simple, we borrowed their aircraft from time to time and woe betide us if we damaged it in any way by our foolishness or inexperience. Although they disclaimed emotion, it was they who showed the most anxiety if we were overdue and their joy when we returned after each operation was incapable of being hidden. They and all like them were superb.

The evening air was cold enough to cut down any lengthy attempts at conversation, Sid seemed anxious to board and get the early checks done since we were the first away. Almost mechanically, Jock, Phil, Peewee and I moved down to the tailwheel and ceremonially relieved our bladders over it. Yet another superstition. Relieved in one sense we climbed aboard and settled ourselves down in our various parts of the aircraft, stowing parachutes and plugging in to the intercom as we went. Moving around the front of the aircraft was going to be slightly more difficult as the second pilot's seat now bridged across the forward passage way leading to the wireless operator and bomb aimer, which meant a dip and a duck every time.

I gave Sid the first course to be flown which he transferred to the main compass and returned to my own 'office' to run over previous calculations. Apprehension had completely vanished, we were now operational. Jock, Phil and Peewee confirmed that all was in order in their turrets and Fitz then checked over the 'works' with Sid.

Another look at my wrist chronometer. Time to start up. Sid gave silent commands with his hands and the groundcrews went into their normal drill. One by one the big Merlin engines burst into life to be joined like some huge Chinese cracker by similar explosions on other sides of the aerodrome. D for Donald began to tremble, sometimes I thought with anticipation. Final engine checks done we peered into the gloom to pick up the duty pilots signal from the control hut near the runway. The correct flash from the Aldis lamp and Sid signalled for 'Chocks away'. We rumbled majestically around the perimeter and stood at the end of the runway all eyes looking for the green light. There it is and with it a lusty roar as D for Donald leapt forward snarling defiance at the Third Reich and gently leaving Lincolnshire for the upper air.

# CHAPTER TWO

# Down

The ground had hardly slipped away before I made sure that the oxygen supply to my mask was working. Another vital matter, because Sid's sinus trouble would have to go by the board. We would have to be well over oxygen height before we cleared the Alps. The oxygen smelt a little stale, mixed as it was with facial perspiration on the mask, and I quickly pulled the mask so that it hung solely on one button; the microphone which was incorporated would always be held over the mouth if I needed to pass a message.

Pushing my way past Fitz's engineer's area I could spasmodically make out the odd light on the ground through the second pilot's side window. This was going to be no joy at all trying to pick up landmarks with the bulk of a second 'dickey' blotting out most of the window space. Sid banked the aircraft and the single line of runway lights came into view and the familiar flashing beacon monotonously winking out the airfield code.

The aircraft straightened up and Sid looked over, pointing to his mask. I lumbered to the navigation table and plugged in:

'Hallo, Captain, Navigator here.'

Sid's voice came back loud and strong: 'Hallo, Navigator. On course. What's our ETA at Dungeness?'

I didn't need to look at my flight plan. '19.31, and we should be at 8,000 feet, climbing from there to 12,000.' I smiled to myself. Sid would stay below 10,000 feet until the last minute. I went on: 'Cloud should be about 5/10ths and we should get a good pinpoint.'

'Okay, Navigator. Keep me informed of any wind changes.'

Jock and Phil piped up on the intercom together both asking about gun testing.

Sid's voice was brisk: 'One at a time. Watch your intercom procedure. You can test the guns over the Channel not before. Wait for my command.' Sid was doing a good training run in front of the sprog. To mollify Jock I asked him to see if he could get me a drift bearing using his turret to follow a ground feature or light and reading off a scale before him. There was rarely a hundred per cent blackout in wildest Lincolnshire and there was always something on which to get a bearing. I didn't really need it so early in the flight but it gave Jock something to do; he called up later to give me the aircraft's drift which tallied perfectly with the calculated one. So far so good. We crossed the western corner of the Wash with East Anglia spread out before us. There were plenty of beacons, and what looked to be quite a lot of ground activity on the airfields of 3 Group who were joining us in the party.

Phil broke the silence to inform Sid that a Lancaster had passed below us on the port beam. Good luck, son, I breathed. There would be more than a few in a quarter of an hour's time.

Cambridge was somewhere away to starboard but fairly anonymous in the blackness, and a little later Chelmsford slipped by. Ahead the first glimmer of the Thames and the bulky twins of the Isle of Grain and the Isle of Sheppey where we had spent some uncomfortable days during the Battle of Britain operating our Fairey Battles against the Channel ports. We were at height now and fairly skimming along over the Kent downs, feeling a sense of history and the aura of victory which the fighter boys had left behind them, and which we were hopefully carrying on our steadily mounting raids against the enemy.

The night's wind was certainly in our favour because we hadn't wavered from our pre-selected track and we were hitting all the landmarks spot on. Dungeness proved to be no different and apart from cries of discovery from the gunners as they confirmed the position, we slipped into the darkness of the Channel, a sinister shape on a sinister errand with the first butterflies beginning to take form in the stomachs of the crew members and the dryness of the throat calling for a hasty sip of whatever was contained in the crew flasks.

From now on the chips were down and everyone was on the look-out for the slightest sign of danger, or anything that was not germane to the normal conduct of the aircraft in flight. All nerve endings were vibrating and each one was mentally alert to the highest degree. The second pilot passed down the aircraft to make the first visit to the 'tube', a pipe and funnel device for errant bladders. The pipe leading to the outside of the aircraft dispensed its contents freely and impartially. Apprehension maybe, first trips were especially edgy, but no one would rib him about it. He would be that much more on his toes when the dull ache had gone.

'Captain to all gunners. You may now test guns. Short bursts only.' Sid was continuing his training routine impeccably. The French coast would be coming up soon and there was no point in giving our position away to any roaming nightfighters. Jock, Phil and Peewee went through their test drills and reported that all was in order, their gunfire was hardly noticeable against the pulsing roar of the four Merlins just a few feet away. Sid checked the estimated time of arrival at the French coast with me and reminded all the crew not to use the intercom unnecessarily. We were flying in and out of cloud now but it was still sufficiently broken to pick up a landfall. Someone ahead had run into some light anti-aircraft fire, probably the gun cover for the airfield at Le Tréport. I called Sid:

'Hallo, Captain, Navigator here. Do you want a course to avoid the flak ahead? We could cross slightly north of Le Tréport.'

He was very calm and in control. 'No. We'll keep to track given. You'll get a similar reception anywhere along this part of the coast.'

Woolly looked round the edge of his partition smiling broadly. Sid wasn't one for dodging hot spots. Peewee's drawl came booming into the earphones:

'Front gunner to navigator. Coastline ahead, could be anywhere.'

Before I could reply, Sid ordered the crew to keep their eyes peeled for a pinpoint, vague remarks like Peewee's sometimes got up his nose. It wasn't necessary in the end; one of the leading aircraft had been coned with searchlights through the gaps in the cloud and the reflected light was enough for us to confirm that we were definitely on course for Le Tréport.

Minutes later we were being buffeted by the German gunners with Sid threading his way through the glowing streaks of cannon fire, deceptively slow until they suddenly burst past you in savage swift arcs cracking and thudding their exploding pieces against anything that dared use the same airspace. Weaving through with careful skill Sid waited until the noise had abated somewhat, checked his course with me and that everyone was all right.

'Keep a constant lookout gunners. This is nightfighter country.'

His command, though accepted, was really superfluous. I could guarantee that those three lads were pushing their eyeballs out on sticks!

Cloud began to thicken as the coast began to recede into the distance. Ice would be the hazard until we passed through the frontal system laying across mid-France, already we could see cloud ahead building up to several thousand feet above us.

'Captain to Navigator, I'm climbing up to just below 10,000 feet.'

Woolly appeared around his partition smiling again. I think he had in mind that Sid would quite likely find a route through the moutains rather than tempt his sinuses.

'Navigator to Captain. Alter course at the new height to 135 degrees.' Sid would tell me when he had levelled out and I was quite sure that he would be sticking to the laid down route tonight. Rain was forming on the windscreen and we were well into cloud now; this was the time when you entered the unknown, nothing apart from the instruments to tell you what lay ahead. You just prayed that no other aircraft was in your vicinity; the uncertainty heightened the suspense and tongues felt uncomfortable in dry mouths.

Happily the cloud level in our area reached only 9,500 feet and we broke cloud into clear air with a thin rim of moon showing bleakly above. Great! If there was any trouble we could always slip quickly back into cloud. By the look of things ahead we might have to climb over another ridge of cloud but there was some time to go yet. No one was offering any resistance from the ground below apart from the occasional individual searchlight under the cloud base, and the Midi of France stretched interminably on. Ample time for recalculation and musing on the upliftment you were giving to the French people, the audible sound of the engines telling them that the struggle to free them was continuing. Lulled by the ease and quietness of the journey we drifted on, revelling in our luck to have clicked for a 'doddle'. The attack when it came was sudden and incisive.

An incandescent missile zinged across the navigation table and ricocheted off the thick steel panel between my position and the wireless operator's compartment. At the same time the aircraft gave a series of shudders and began to yaw to port, in a slow diving turn. The angle made it difficult for me to rise to see what was happening and as I pulled myself upright using one of the fuselage stanchions I heard Sid broadcasting to the crew in measured tones that the aircraft had been attacked and that the port engines and wing were on fire. He was losing height in an attempt to put the fire out.

'We will be able to maintain height on two engines but standby to abandon aircraft if need be.'

It all seemed pretty well under control, but there had been no warning or word from the gunners. I moved up to the pilot's position leaving Fitz to assist in the closing down of the engines and the extinguishing of the engine fires.

The front cabin was brilliantly illuminated by the flames and

Sid's grim silhouette was bent over the controls; he was glancing over at the second pilot and obviously passing commands in a desperate effort to keep us in the air. The dive to port became steeper and I reached for one of the forward intercom sockets to plug in for any order affecting me. The immediate priority was to get on an even keel, navigation would have to remain in abeyance, but I would have to have a course ready for us to fly a return leg home. Before I could connect the plug Fitz hammered on my back and pulled the side flap of my helmet away.

'We've got to bale out!' he shouted against the roaring whine outside.

My intercom plug went home and I could hear Sid's voice high and strident:

'Abandon aircraft. Abandon aircraft. Immediately.'

I pushed my way under the second pilot and saw below me Woolly and Peewee crouching round the escape hatch, parachutes already attached and helmets off. The angle of the aircraft was becoming steeper by the second. I tore my helmet and scarf off and lurched towards the crouching pair and Peewee cupped his hand over my ear.

'The bloody hatch is jammed,' he was screaming.

Woolly pushed Peewee to one side and sat on the floor just before the hatch and gave an almighty kick; it needed about three but it eventually flew out. Moving behind them and pushing over to where my own and Fitz's parachute was stowed I watched them both disappear into the night. I clipped on my own chute and clawed my way to the hatch to discover in a blinding flash of horror that I had clipped it on upside down, I could see myself clawing away for the rip ring with the wrong hand. It had to be unclipped and put round the right way.

Fractions of a second were passing and I held on to Woolly's seat reclipping whilst Fitz got his chute and bent by the escape hatch. He would have gone but parachute drill was ingrained in us all, Woolly out first, then Peewee, then me, then Fitz. He waited, and I rolled to the hatch looking back into the pilot's compartment with its eerie bright red light, Sid's stony face almost gargoyle-like and Sergeant Wood's wide open eyes above a countenance serious with concentration. Fitz tapped my head and put his thumb up. I sat over the hatch, dropped my legs outside in a tremendously tugging slipstream, placed my right hand round the rip ring and went. The change to complete silence was immediate and I turned over in a cartwheel feeling the dampness of cloud all about me. Semi-consciously counting I pulled the rip ring as if in training.

The damp cloud was still all around me as I swung first one way then the other. I felt a little sick and realised that my head and face were aching badly. It then dawned on me what had happened. I had looked down when pulling the rip ring instead of turning my head to one side and my face had taken the full force of the opening parachute clipped to my chest which had knocked me unconscious. Stupid thing to do, my neck ached as well.

Peering down at my feet I could see no breaks in the cloud, I was floating it seemed for ages in a strange silent world getting wetter all the time and beginning to feel the cold eating through my Sidcot suit. Then, as if by magic, the cloud disappeared and the dark earth lay below, an odd light showing here and there. No way of telling what sort of area I would land in, I would have to trust to luck. It was coming up pretty fast now and as the last few feet dissolved, I felt a fresh flash of pain as I finally made contact.

*

Rain was steadily dripping down the neck of my Sidcot helping me back to consciousness again. The pain in my head and neck had been joined by some in my legs. I pressed my eyelids together and lifted up my face to the rain, discovering at the same time that I was still swinging to and fro. The pressure on my armpits indicated that I was still on the end of my parachute, but surely I remembered meeting the ground? I strained my eyes to see what I could pick up in the murk, and gradually made out tree shapes everywhere. Up above I could see my parachute canopy hanging limply over a maze of branches. So that was it! I had hit a wood or forest and managed to fall through one of the trees, knocking myself out again! Looking down was more difficult, the blackness there made it impossible to tell what terrain lay concealed but it seemed to me that I was not very far from terra firma. There was no point remaining where I was so I reached for the release button on the parachute harness and fell and fell and fell. A sickening thud and I was back in the comfort of unconsciousness for the third time that night.

I must have lain there for quite a while before I opened my eyes again, feeling strangely comfortable almost as if I was supported by a giant hand. Rain was falling directly onto my face with a stinging sensation which made me raise my hand to discover the cause. I was obviously cut but how badly was impossible to tell. It was then that I remembered the fall and I tried to sit up to take stock of the situation. Pain came back in swift waves but I was moving my limbs and no bones seemed to be broken. The giant hand turned out to be the gnarled roots of the tree I had crashed through and across which I was unceremoniously draped. Pain or not I was getting up and after a series of agonising contortions I finished up at an angle of 45 degrees holding onto the tree trunk for dear life.

Whatever lay ahead I would be needing a boost, and a couple of caffeine tablets from the escape kit I was carrying might just do that. It took a lot of will at that moment to twist around so that my back was against the tree, and this gave me my first feeling of satisfaction after the nightmare of the descent. Reaching the zipper of the Sidcot suit was another milestone and at least my arms, although aching, were working all right. Bracing myself I lifted out the package containing the escape kit which I had stowed inside my battledress top, and carefully took out the map printed on silk. This would be invaluable later on and I tucked it inside the top pocket of the battledress. The kit was carefully packed: fortified chocolate, water purifying tablets, caffeine tablets, vitamin pills, hard biscuit all neatly in compartments.

There was enough rain dripping down my face to make the swallowing of the caffeine extremely easy. It would take some time to react, but psychologically I was kidding myself that I could start to move off from the scene right away and somehow I managed to stumble to the next tree. Oh boy!! It took a while until I was ready to move on but strength returned and the trees were slowly passing by. The Germans would, no doubt, be already looking for the crew if the aircraft had crashed nearby and I needed to be as far away from that hanging parachute as I could.

Soft leaves underfoot kept me from jarring my bones too much but they kept me from realising that I had no boot on my left foot and this was brought violently home to me when I kicked against another gnarled root. Sinking down in despair, I rested against the adjacent tree trunk to ponder the problem. Something had to go round my foot if I was to have any chance at all. The bulk of my Mae West produced the answer although I was reluctant to use it as it had been a good friend to me. The lumpy pad at the back of my neck had undoubtedly helped to protect my head during the fall, as had the chest pads, and if I were forced to stay out in open country it would make an excellent pillow.

Compromise was the answer and I decided to cut out one of the

**Right** Myself aged 18 in July 1939 on entry into the RAF.

**Below** Fairey Battles, the aircraft I flew in during the Battle of France (*Norman Franks*).

**Above** With 12 Squadron at Stainton-le-Vale, Lincolnshire, in late 1940, at the Manor House where aircrew were dispersed from the airfield for safety reasons. I am fifth from the left, top row.

**Below** With my crew, 12 Squadron, at Binbrook in early 1941. Left to right: Paddy Taylor, George Jolley, Mickey Finnis, P/O Bairstow, myself, and Peter Tracey (not the crew I was with on the night of 24–25 October 1942).

chest pads, offering up a prayer of thanksgiving for having remembered to stow a large clasp knife in one of my Sidcot pockets. It wasn't easy in the gloom of the forest floor and I wouldn't take any tailoring prizes but the pad came away at last. Making a big enough slit in the outer covering I pushed my foot in amongst the buoyancy material.

Bending my leg to do so gave me another jolt of pain in my lower back but I kept it bent whilst I cut off one of the cloth straps of the Mae West and tied it roughly round the pad and my ankle. It was just long enough. Somebody was looking after me! Another painful set of movements and I was upright, resting against the tree. It felt OK and confidence came pouring in. Most of my previous aches around the head had dulled by now; whatever trouble I was in was coming from the lower back although I could walk after a fashion without it hurting too much. The next few yards confirmed that with care the pad was going to stay on my foot and unbelievably I began to increase speed without any significant effort. Of course, my brain shouted, you must be going downhill, and I stumbled on half laughing and half crying hardly caring what was in the way. The uppermost thought recurring in my mind was to get the hell out of there and to find some sort of help and shelter.

Anyone who has run through a dark forest in their dreams will know exactly how it was, and I cannot describe the overwhelming sense of relief that I felt as the darkness began to pale. I broke through the last of the trees and stood in a steeply sloping meadow; there was sufficient light for me to make out a gate on the far side. Standing there on my wobbly legs I tried to take it all in. From now I had to be careful and the next objective was to get to that gate unseen. Crouching as far as the pain would allow me I moved crab fashion across the field stopping from time to time but eventually throwing myself on the gate for support. It was then that I realised I was making a fearful noise breathing in loud raucous gasps. I hung there getting my breath back slowly, hoping that no one could hear me.

It stayed quiet and soon I was able to raise my head straining my eyes to find my bearings. For one thing the rain had stopped. I was also still on sloping ground with several fields below me. A long thin ribbon shining in the half light lay behind the fields and was punctuated by dark lumps which could have been trees or perhaps houses. An odd light was visible in the area suggesting some sort of civilisation.

Time to go. I needed to get down further to make sure of my next move. The gate was chained up and I tried to swing my right leg up to climb over it. It just wouldn't lift up and the effort was agonising. There was not time to find a gap in the hedge so I leant over the gate as far as I could and toppled to the ground on the other side. It didn't help matters but I had been lucky and there was no extra reaction from my back. Using the gate for support I scrambled back upright and took the cart track from the gate keeping to the hedge for cover. The pad on my left foot was bearing up well. My flying boot must have been sucked off when I made the jump; a pity but perhaps I could put that right if I could reach a friendly house and get some better footwear.

The next two fields offered no problem as the gates were closed only by a metal loop. The thin ribbon I had seen from the upper field appeared to be a road and there looked to be quite a number of houses along it, one or two showing a light. An ARP warden would have a field day here, I thought, but I suppose since this is somewhere in mid-France no one is too bothered. Another field, but this one still had animals in it, could be cattle but I wasn't staying to find out. Lowering myself on my back I rolled underneath the boundary hedge into the field beyond. Empty, it seemed.

I stood up again clutching the hedge on the way and lurched down to the lower end of the slope. A low hedge confronted me but over the top of it I could make out a wooden hut. Glory be! If I could get in I could pass the night there. I felt exhausted.

A light suddenly came on and some children's voices pierced the night air, and I could see that the light came from further down from a dwelling. I was actually looking into a garden and a door had been opened to allow the children out, probably to put a pet in an outhouse. Perhaps the family would help me?

There was no gap in the hedge but moving to my left I found another gate in the field corner, this one chained up. Fortunately there was a gap between the gatepost and the hedge and I pushed through desperately. A short track lay before me, and the road I had seen lay at the end of it. I could still hear the high-pitched voices of the children as I made my way gingerly to the end of the track. There were houses either side and across the road too. It had the appearance of a large village but I reached the road with no one in sight. I needed help badly. Which house do I try? The children's voices had come from the house on my right. Okay old son, I said to myself this is where we leave it in the hands of the angels. Rain was still dripping down the door as I reached it. There was no knocker or post flap. Bunching my knuckles I gave three raps and prayed that I was right.

Seconds passed without any sign from inside. Was this the house with the children in it? I looked again up and down the road, no one in sight. Feeling completely exposed with a latent fear beginning to rise within me I hammered once again on the wet wood. The door opened slowly to reveal a husband and wife in their thirties, eyes wide open with astonishment, incredulity and incomprehension. I could see a passage behind them with an open door at the end through which young children in their bedclothes were peering. The couple and I stared at each other for a moment.

Finally, '*Que veut tu?*' from the man. He was holding his wife's shoulders as if I were some visiting demon.

'*Je suis un aviateur anglais. Je suis tombé par parachute près d'ici.*' My school French came tumbling out urgently. '*J'ai besoin d'assistance.*'

The man released his wife and pulled me into the house. I was about to drop and he realised this and guided me to a chair. The warmth of the room and the obvious concern of the couple were comforting after the anguish of the last few hours and I felt as if I were a little intoxicated. I was babbling and rambling on to them that I had been in France two years earlier with the RAF and that if I could get to Paris I could make contact with the Resistance movement.

The woman placed her hand on my mouth and motioned to me to be silent. She went off and came back with a bowl and some cloth and began to bathe my face. It stang a little but not as badly as it had previously. She followed that up with a most soothing ointment applied with great tenderness as if I were one of her own. Finished, she fetched a large mirror and I stared at myself in amazement. I had four diagonal cuts across my forehead and face, either made by the opening parachute or by the branches of the tree I had landed in. No wonder they had been so taken aback when the door had opened. I looked really evil. She lowered the mirror smiled and said something I did not understand. Motioning for me to take off my Sidcot she disappeared again to return with a bowl of soup and some bread and cheese. I motioned back to show that I couldn't do it alone and she and her husband pulled me upright and after removing the remains of the Mae West peeled me like a banana. Gently lowering me back to the chair they carefully removed my flying boot and foot pad. The white silk oversocks I was wearing were quite dry and they seemed impressed by them. I was able to introduce the occasional word but mostly we managed in sign language. I wolfed the bread, cheese and soup without a sound.

The man brought in a selection of shoes of various sizes and finally managed to fit me up with a light pair with flimsy soles. Perhaps they wouldn't stand up to a lot of walking but they were a great advance on what I had arrived in. He motioned to the insignia on my battle dress blouse and produced some scissors. If I was going to be seen outside it was common sense to make myself as inconspicuous as possible. The RAF blue was going to be bad enough but my gear was well worn and scruffy. I waved him to go ahead and he neatly clipped off my wing, medal ribbon and warrant officer's badge and threw them on the fire. Quizzically he looked at the metal badge of the French Tank Corps sewn on the right breast pocket of my battledress.

'*Les Chars d'Assau,*' he asserted.

'*Oui,*' I replied. '*Un souvenir de quarante.*'

He nodded, satisfied. Taking the scissors from him I snipped it off myself and dropped in in my breast pocket. '*Pour bonne chance.*' I smiled.

He nodded again but he was becoming increasingly nervous shooting glances at the door of the room as if he expected trouble. I lifted the escape kit from the Sidcot pocket I had used and took out a wad of French banknotes. He was completely nonplussed and waved his arms in refusal, quietly calling out to his wife. She came back hurriedly and after a brief exchange of words pushed my hand back towards me.

'*Non, non.*' She was insistent.

'*Oui,*' I persevered. '*C'est un cadeau de Churchill. Pour les enfants.*'

Something inside her made her see that this was no ordinary gift. I peeled off a couple of the highest value notes and our hands closed in acceptance, unsaid thanks being understood. The couple exchanged some more phrases and the man was obviously anxious to see me go.

'*Allez maintenant,*' he said in a slow direct tone.

I held up my hand. They had done far more than I could have expected but one thing remained to be discovered. Producing the silk map from my breast pocket I stood up slowly and placed it on the table spreading it out under the dim light. Raising my hands in a questioning posture I demanded '*Où?*' pointing at the map. Both sets of eyes lit up and the couple leant on the table indicating the position of their village.

'*Ligny-en-Barrois*,' said the man. '*Allez maintenant.*'

It was time to make tracks. I put my hands on their shoulders and we passed into the passage outside. They were plainly frightened and I did not wish to prolong their discomfort.

'*Au revoir*,' I mumbled, my lips beginning to quiver with emotion. Expecting them to open the door to the road outside I moved toward it. A touch on my shoulder and I turned to see them beckoning to a side door from the passage. I should have known better, they were taking unholy chances in giving me help or refuge and their lives hung on a slender thread if it became known that they had aided a British flyer. Anyone passing along the road would instantly have been suspicious at that time of night with curfews rigidly applied throughout Occupied France. I was to slip out of the house as if I were a wanted person, and in truth that is just what I was. The side door opened and I turned to them with a heart filled with gratitude. The man just waved his head from side to side and handed me a flat cap.

'*Bonne chance*' were his final words.

# CHAPTER THREE

# The Long Walk

Clutching my escape kit I stepped out into the night stiff but mobile; the soup had really made a difference. The scene was familiar and I realised that I was back on the track between the houses, the side door behind me was pretty concealed. I must have missed seeing it when I passed by before. It was deathly quiet and the obvious thing was to make my way around the back of the village to look for a decent resting place. Turning back up the track I reached the first gate and again squeezed through the gap into the field.

The exertion was making my heart beat alarmingly and the effort of climbing uphill was bringing back the devils in my back. Truly I wasn't going to get very far. Skirting the hedge on the lower slope of the field I found it was flatter and easier so I kept to that and passed several houses, there seemed no end to them. Another hedge loomed up dead across my path. The end of the field, but what lay beyond? There was a small gap underneath it and I got down once again into a supine position and eased my way underneath resting on my good hip. With a muffled cry I rolled down a small bank and lay there panting and feeling rough. I was at the edge of a small road; a house lay on the other side with a low white boundary fence, and I rose up and staggered over to it. Praise be, I could make out a shed some way from the house.

It looked very much as if I would have to do my toppling act again if I was to get over the fence but as luck would have it I found a gate first. It squealed like a pig as it was opened and I froze in alarm. No one came to investigate and loosening my tongue from the roof of my mouth, I eased through the gateway without attempting to open the gate any further. There remained a short, flagged path and blowing slightly I made my way as quietly as I could to the shed thankful that the shoes I had been given were ideal for the purpose, supple and squeakless, a boon to a fugitive.

Amazingly there was no lock on the shed door, just a simple wooden block in a socket. Pulling it across I opened up tentatively, no squeaking this time and passed inside amongst lengths of wood and all the smells of a carpenter's trade. The small window gave a little light and I felt around for a while along the surrounding benches, filled with tools and tins. There was no chance of a comfortable night on a bench, so I quietly cleared a space on the floor and sank down to immediate oblivion.

The clatter of a heavy vehicle shot me out of sleep. Thin light was filtering into the shed and I could see the roof timbers clearly. My nervous alarm system must have been automatically activated because I was aware instantly of my predicament and the events of the previous night. Lying on my back I felt quite fresh and I lifted up my left arm to check my wrist chronometer. It was just after 5 a.m., probably 6 a.m. in France. Getting up was more difficult than I imagined, every joint seemed to have stiffened up but, with the aid of a trestle, I was soon erect and reasonably steady. My mouth was a little dry but I could look for water later; the first priority was to move off now.

The map last night had shown the village to be one point of a triangle with the small towns of Bar-le-Duc and St Dizier as the other points. If any of the crew were about I might meet up with them in that triangle so I decided to head for Bar-le-Duc first and then St Dizier. There was no point in being furtive. With my scruffy battledress and flat cap it would be best to stick to the main roads as if I were a country worker. Hardly had I settled that in my mind than I was gripped by bowel pains and it became urgently necessary to relieve them. Probably brought on by jangling nerves! The trestle was handy and lowering my trousers I sat on top of it. It was no legacy to leave a good Frenchman whose hospitality I had abused, but if ever I met up with him in the future I hoped that he would forgive me. Leaving the shed hurriedly and making my way back to the gate in the half light, I ran my hands through the tall grass at the road-side and sucked greedily at the dew drops. This would have to do until I found a stream.

The road to the right led back into the village to join the main road. Happily for me, my leg muscles were coming back to normal. There was no chance that I was going to walk properly but the limp I had affected to take the weight off my right hip might suggest that I was disabled in some way and not good material for forced labour. It remained to be seen, but it was tested soon enough for as I reached the corner two German soldiers passed in front of me on their way back into the village. They hardly spared me a glance, and I turned the opposite way with considerable elation. Before me stretched a straight road over a gentle rise and one or two local people were moving about with hand carts and bags in a slow, sleepy tempo.

It was getting lighter, and as the houses slowly petered out I could make out on the wall of one of them a chiselled out road sign 'Bar-le-Duc 16 km'. So I was on the right road, but the prospect of a ten-mile walk was daunting. Maybe I wouldn't make St Dizier. I stopped at a clump of trees, waited until the road was clear and popped a couple of caffeine tablets in my mouth. It was difficult to get them down but some dew on the roadside grass helped a little. They were supposed to keep you awake I thought, and then smiled as I remembered the immediate slumber in the shed. I took another and started off again keeping to the left hand side of the road to face any oncoming people or vehicles.

Topping a rise, I met up with two German patrols about a hundred yards between them, marching back into Ligny-en-Barrois. Keeping to one side as they passed, I couldn't understand why they were not interested in anyone if there had been a hue and cry the previous evening, but I was thankful that my ruse to keep out in the open seemed to be working and that I was reasonably anonymous.

The temperature was surprisingly warm and there was little cloud. I felt able to move at a good pace and the first few kilometres went by quite quickly. More carts and vehicles were moving about but the villagers of Velaines and later Tronville-en-Barrois were going about their business in a sullen way and paying no attention to itinerant scruffs. Thirst was making itself felt and it was going to be important to keep up a water intake. Luckily a stream crossed the road just before the next village and I was able to rest on the bank and cup my hands for the precious liquid. Remembering after the first long and deep draught, I fished out of the escape kit a purifying tablet which took a short while to dissolve in the water I had cupped the second time. Whatever else it did, it made the taste unpalatable and I resolved to trust to luck instead. Refreshed, I noticed on the side of the little bridge a white stone saying 'Bar-le-Duc 8 km'. I could hardly believe it. Halfway already! Into the escape kit, this time for a piece of the chocolate. Fortified it certainly was, hard, thick and very strong tasting, but it was going to be my life-line for a time.

Back on the road the first German transport appeared, mostly wagons with the odd guard peering from the back. An occasional motorcyclist roared by and then lo and behold a Heinkel 111 appeared over the hills flanking the road. For a brief moment I stood in wonder and deep interest but quickly realised that folks thereabouts were by then used to the sight and sound of things

German and I was exhibiting undue curiosity, not the thing to do if I were to be undiscovered. It was about this time, probably because of stopping, that it became obvious that my shoes were beginning to feel the strain. One sole was lifting away from the upper; limping along was putting a severe strain on the flimsy construction. Slowly does it then; thank goodness the road was fairly flat. The sun was getting up and the scenery was quite pretty, I felt vaguely tired but the caffeine was working well.

After what seemed an age I reached Longueville with five and a half kilos to go. Traffic was becoming steady and more aeroplanes hove into view. A little further on and the reason was clear, I was skirting the aerodrome outside Bar-le-Duc. Making a mental note of what I could see in the way of number of aircraft and types, I pressed on into the outskirts of the town. Fatigue was beginning to get to me and I recognised that for the last kilometre or two I had been moving automatically without really appreciating my surroundings. A rest was again paramount and I kept an eye out for somewhere suitable. Unhappily the area through which I was passing became more and more built up and as I got nearer to the centre of the town the numbers of German servicemen moving about grew alarmingly and I felt that there was no point in trying to find help there, it was far too dangerous.

A minor crossroads gave me the opportunity I needed. A sign in German script said 'St Dizier 25 km' and I turned away from the town in a daze, feeling fairly faint. The road led through a dormitory part of the town and soon became an uphill route out into the country. Time just went past and I must have lapsed into semi-consciousness because I woke up to find myself at another crossroads with the sign to St Dizier on my left recording 22 kilometres.

I sank down in the ditch at the side of the road and gave up for a while. Later I came round to find that I had slipped down into the brackish water at the ditch bottom, the foot with the cracked shoe had just broken the surface and felt soggy and uncomfortable. I huddled at the side of the water and cupped it up in frenzied gulps. My leg was unaccountably bending without too much pain now and I pulled myself to road level to see who was about. Not a soul. I lay on my back and had some more caffeine, chocolate and biscuit.

A stroke of good fortune came my way as I went to get my knife to break the chocolate. Out of my pocket with the knife came the cloth strap I had used to fasten the Mae West chest pad to my foot the previous night. It must have been tucked away absentmindedly when I was being helped by the couple at Ligny. It held the cracked shoe together beautifully and I tied it so that I could move it again if the piece under the sole wore away. Heartened by this godsend I lifted myself back onto the road and began walking again.

The sun sat high above my head and I stole a glance at my wrist chronometer. Just after midday then, and doing just about two miles an hour. Not at all bad in the circumstances. What concerned me was that I had not seen any of the lads en route and I wandered along wondering about their fate. The road began to climb again and I steeled myself for a long hike to the next village. The incline began to take its toll and by the time I had reached the top I had slowed to a jerky shuffle. There was no sign of any travellers or vehicles, the whole business seemed most eerie when compared with the heavy bustle of the road into Bar-le-Duc. Maybe it was lunchtime. I didn't care; in fact I began not to care about anything for weariness was beginning to pervade my entire body. My lips were dry and I had a flashback in my mind of a scene from a film set in the desert with the hero staggering across the sand-dunes trying to find an oasis. The ditches at the roadside here were dry; like the hero I would have to push on despite the fact that I was getting very light-headed. Lack of food and drink and the warm sun weren't assisting my cause.

The village of Brillon came in sight and I roused myself from my lethargic plodding in an effort to get there. Another rest was necessary and perhaps someone there would take pity on me. Very dry and more than a little dusty I finally made it to the village centre. Knowing that I was beaten, that my feet hurt and quite a bit elsewhere hurt, I was in the right mood to surrender to whatever authorities were around. A notice over one building proclaimed 'Mairie' and from my previous days in France I knew this to be the local Mayor's office. It was ideal, and felt gloriously cool as I hobbled inside. Holding onto a high counter for support and swaying slightly I waited whilst an old gnarled French lady bandied words with an obese monster of a woman in black behind the counter. Their words shrilled to a high crescendo and the monster's face grew dark red under what aspired to be a fuzzy beard.

They paid no attention to me whatever and the longer I hung there on the counter the more my reason was returning. Suddenly it occurred to me that the last thing I wanted to do was to give myself up. The harangue lapsed into silence and the old lady flung a last vitriolic sentence towards the counter and strutted out onto the street. She never knew that I came out right behind her.

The sunlight was bright in my eyes after the dark coolness of the Mairie, but not enough for me to avoid seeing an open church door opposite. A few children were running in and out but they made way for me almost in awe, as I tottered over the doorstep. Like the Mairie it was shaded and cool inside, very basic, rows of pews and a few ornaments. A plain altar was topped by a simple wooden cross. No priest was in attendance; if there had been I am sure he would have done something about the children gambolling down the aisle and round the pews. I dropped into a pew and tried to think of what to do next. St Dizier was a good ten miles away, or was it twenty or fifty? Thoughts, mostly unconnected, were drifting through my mind in quick succession and my consciousness was going.

I felt the hard pew under my shoulders and jerked upwards. The church was silent, the children had gone and I was alone sensing the sanctitude of the place mingled with stale odours. My early upbringing in the Boy's Brigade came to my aid here and I sent up a silent prayer for help. The answer came with startling clarity. Go on to St Dizier and get help in the church there. I checked the time; I had been out for an hour and a half. Well, if He was going to help, ten miles wouldn't be too much of a hurdle. Pulling myself together I went out into the bright sunlight again, hoping to find something to drink as I went along. The rest had done me good in a sense but I was very much the worse for wear. Sheer determination to get to St Dizier was going to be the driving force.

Outside the village the road began to descend and at first I was terribly elated but then realisation came over me that I would have to climb later on. This almost broke my new found determination until after a few hundred yards I could see ahead the village of Sandrupt and the river running through it. Here was the chance for a brief rest and a long cool drink, and so it came to pass in an idyllic spot underneath a bridge with attendant ducks and water birds. Far too crafty by now to call attention to myself I desisted from feeding them, but selfishly as it seemed wolfed most of the remaining food in the escape kit, keeping a small reserve for the next seven miles. I could have lain there for ever, I think; I had walked all the pain out of my body and mind, although I knew that it was there somewhere in the background.

Rising again reluctantly, I hurried as best I could through the village and up into the wooded hills beyond. It definitely felt better going up this rise; my mind was clearer, my breathing was hardly noticeable and maybe I had a clearer goal than previously. A long stretch soon passed under my feet and I looked back on Sandrupt with some sense of achievement. The way ahead seemed much flatter and still there was no sign of traffic. I had waved at the odd cart but this must surely be one of the most deserted tracts in France. Even a main crossroads with five miles to go offered nothing in the way of movement in any direction. Tiredness was returning but I fought it off for a kilometre or two before deciding to look for another resting place. It came shortly after passing through Chancenay, where a little more in the way of vehicles was present. Small German open cars were in evidence and a number of villagers were strung out in a line as if watching a race.

I passed by without much interest being displayed in me, and ran into several groups of children further up the road, all in an excited mood. It crossed my mind that it was probably a similar situation as in England when school or Sunday School sports are held. Smiling, I weaved through them and disappeared around the bend of the road. Ditches were quite deep on each side and I slid into one to recuperate, but before I could close my eyes I caught the sound of gravel crunching on the road. Hugging the rough side of the ditch in sheer desperation I waited with misgiving.

'*Monsieur*,' a childish voice said.

I stared in disbelief at the little face above. It was one of the children from the village. Choking back my relief I placed my finger across my lips. I remembered the French word for thirst. '*Soif*,' I croaked, and put my finger back across my lips to emphasise the secrecy I needed. His dear little head nodded and he disappeared to reappear almost immediately with an apple.

'*Merci*', was all that I could give him. Money might have complicated matters. He stood above me as I consumed the apple, practically in one piece. Wearing an amused expression he watched me crawl out of the ditch. It would be dangerous to stay any longer.

I patted his head, smiled and turned away, unable to keep my tears from flowing. What prompted him to do what he did I would never know but it was a gentle, compassionate and kindly deed I would always remember.

There was no further chance to take a rest and I hurried on to get a bit of distance between me and Chancenay in case the lad had found it impossible to keep the secret. In any event the sight and sound of more German transport was increasing my desire to finish the walk and get shelter for the night, and the tiredness creeping back in my bones was being kept in abeyance because of my heightened nervous tension. Telegraph pole after telegraph pole finally gave way to houses and sheds and I was in the outskirts of the town of St Dizier with evening coming on. Shortly after I reached the main crossroads in the town itself, chock-a-block with all manner of vehicles including tanks. Heavy fuel smells fouled the air and I passed quickly over to lose myself amongst the throngs of people in the shopping centre. A church couldn't be very far away so I struck off on tour and found myself in a small square filled with little coloured stalls.

Above the square in the buildings around it I could see German soldiery who were obviously billeted inside. One soldier was cleaning a gun whilst he looked on the scene below from a large open window; he exchanged glances with me frowning as he did so. I darted behind one of the stalls and breathed more easily. Perhaps he had picked out the Air Force blue. I turned into a small alley back into the shopping area and carried on searching. Turning a corner I found myself in the same square and looking up almost automatically found the same soldier peering down. He placed the gun down and walked out of sight but I was giving him no chance of satisfying his curiosity if he came down below. Half running I went through an alley on the opposite side of the square and a few yards away saw a large church standing back a little from the road leading past it. Providence? Maybe, but I wasn't stopping to ponder on it!

Brushing past a number of people who managed to get in my way as I frantically made for a refuge, I eventually stood catching my breath before the heavy wooden door of the church. A look back to the alley from which I had emerged confirmed that there were no pursuers and I composed myself to make a solemn entry. A large iron ring on the door, well smoothed by many previous hands, turned in my hand to release the lock and I gave it as strong a pull as I was capable of providing. The door swung open quickly and quietly to disclose the backs of several German soldiers who turned inquisitively, curious as to the reason for the door opening.

In a fraction of a second I decided to bluff it out, to have moved backwards would, I think, have been fatal to my chances. I moved forward and they parted to let me through into part of the entrance way which still had a few standing places. I knew sufficient about the Catholic faith to cross myself immediately and lowered my head a little to keep anonymity. The church was full to bursting and a hymn struck up. Through it all I mimed furiously, trying to sort out in my mind what I was going to do.

There was little time for that, as it happened. After a brief blessing the organ began again and the priest, officials and the choir began to form for the procession, coming in slow file towards the main entrance where I was standing. The smell of incense was heavy and the strain of the long journey I had made was starting to tell. I had to get help soon or I was certain that I was going to drop in my tracks. If the service ended I would be borne out of the church by the tide of people wanting to get outside and I might not get an opportunity to get back in. The procession reached the entrance area and turned to the right towards some side doors in the transept, the heads of the priest and other adults were just visible over the heads of the three rows of people in front of me.

I am completely at a loss to describe what came over me at that point; probably some innate prehistoric instinct for survival! Whatever it was, it prompted me to push my way through the rows of people to the front, and as the last of the choir boys passed before me I joined the procession behind them. No one made any sound of dissent or disapproval and I continued to follow with bowed head. No doubt I was the subject of conversation between worshippers as they left the church, who may have thought me to be carried away by religious ecstasy, or perhaps to be one of the band of souls who looked after the vestments and the church generally. All I knew was that I was desperate and that the situation had called for desperate measures.

The procession finally arrived at, and went through, the doors in the transept and I found myself in a large room filled with lockers, apparently for the use of the choir boys, since they were already discarding their cassocks and other items in a tumult of shrieks and high spirited chatter. The priest was still amongst them joking and admonishing at the same time and although I tried to capture his attention the boys were milling about him and nobody seemed to accept my presence at all. In fact it wasn't until a number of them had left that I was able to touch the priest's arm and draw him aside. He looked doubtful and apprehensive and taken aback that there was someone other than the procession in the room. He looked even worse when I trotted out my parrot phrase in a hoarse whisper:

'*Je suis un aviateur Anglais. Je suis tombé par parachute près de Ligny-en-Barrois. J'ai besoin d'assistance.*'

Placing his hand over my mouth his eyes entreated for silence, but he saw also my poor physical appearance and with grave care led me by the arm to a long wooden bench. Quickly he was amongst the remaining choirboys cajoling and good-naturedly pushing the last of them from the room. Successful at last he leant against the doors with his back, sighing deeply. Fixing me eventually with a penetrating gaze he came towards me bubbling over with rapid French phrases obviously asking me what in heaven's name I was doing there. The anxiety he was showing was brought on, I assumed, by the close proximity of the German army and I sat there in a haze vaguely sympathising with his fearful mien. The torrent of words stopped and I motioned to him that conversation was hopeless.

'*Je ne parle pas beaucoup Français!*' I managed, leaning back heavily against a wooden support and closing my eyes.

He made sure first that I was safe in my position, I felt his hands on my shoulders as he did so, and he was out and back in the room in a trice bearing a metal cup of water. The cool liquid brought me back to reality and I hunched up on the bench drinking greedily. Then gently the priest lifted up my head and motioned for me to follow him.

Noticing my reluctance, which was really my inability to get back on my feet without a struggle, he came back to place one arm under mine and guiding me with his other arm steered us in ungainly fashion through another door which led onto a staircase. The movement had got my consciousness control operating again and at the foot of the stairs I had recovered enough to indicate to the priest that I could manage the climb if he was close by. For all I was aware we might have been attempting the northern face of the Eiger, it certainly felt like it, but we triumphed and also traversed a long corridor as an encore. The priest pointed at one of the doors leading off.

'*Monsieur L'Abbé,*' he explained, but it wasn't until the door had opened to reveal an aged and venerable priest sitting in an armchair that I understood the term. This must be the chief, I thought.

The priest sat me on a side chair and went over to have a deep and agitated conversation with the Abbé, who then rose and came towards me.

'Good evening, my son.' His warm words with a heavy French inflexion, trickled into my ears, and he picked up my hands and held them with tenderness. 'I speak some English,' he said. 'Can I help you?'

I looked up into his kind wrinkled face and replied wearily, 'I am tired and need food and sleep. My back is hurting.' He spoke quickly to the first priest who hurried away to return with some thick pyjamas.

'You must clean yourself,' advised the Abbé. 'Father Pascal has made a bath.'

I nodded and followed Father Pascal into a large bathroom with a high metal bath in one corner and sloughed off my clothes in an untidy pile. There were one or two painful moments but eventually Father Pascal had pulled off my long-johns and helped me over the high side of the bath. The water was not very warm both because there was very little of it and there had not been much time to boil anything. It was more than enough and I managed to sit there whilst Father Pascal washed all that he could see and then dropped a cloth into the bath for me to complete matters.

The next few moments were extremely dangerous as we struggled to work out a system for getting out of there. A dressing gown belt tied to a window latch overhead finally did the trick, with me heaving myself up and Father Pascal pushing and pulling at anything handy. The bath had done wonders and I stood safely outside it finishing off towelling what Father Pascal hadn't dried. He motioned for me to wait and went off to bring back the Abbé into the bathroom.

Again an agitated conversation and then I felt a touch in my lower right rib cage. A stabbing pain shot through my back and I cried out, holding on to the side of the bath. 'Pardon, my son. You need help to your back,' sympathised the Abbé, 'I will send Father Pascal for someone. Dress for sleeping now and come eat.' The unprofessional examination made the slipping on of pyjama trousers a painful episode but with the aid of a chair Father Pascal managed it and we all made our way back into the Abbé's sitting room.

I suppose that somewhere the Abbé had a cook and housekeeper but there was no sign of her. Father Pascal appeared with a tray of food, broth, bread and some meat-like substance and an apple, and I sat at a small table opposite the Abbé and devoured it, with some very odd-tasting coffee. Father Pascal then made his leave and I began a long and rambling explanation of the activities of the last twenty-four hours.

The Abbé nodded from time to time and I spoke as slowly as I could; he seemed amazed that I had walked 25 miles, or 40 kilometres, that day without being apprehended or questioned. He made it quite clear that I must leave the church the next morning, they were running grave risks in harbouring me, and ran equally as large risks if I were to be caught in due course and made to tell who had given me assistance. They did, however, want to make perfectly sure that I was capable of making my own way and that I had sufficient clothing and food for the immediate future. My eyes were getting heavy but I fought off the unconscious desire my body was expressing for sleep.

What, said the Abbé, did I intend to do when I left? I explained that I was making for Paris where I was sure that there would be organisations to help me. He said that St Dizier was on the line to Paris and that there were workers in the Citroën Factory who travelled daily to Paris on the workers' train. His advice was to travel on this train and to pass through the barriers at the Gare de l'Est in the general press of workers. So far as he knew the workers had never been stopped to have their papers examined. It sounded very plausible. I had enough money left and the Abbé got quite excited when he saw how well aircrews were provided for in terms of escape money. I offered him some which he firmly refused.

A knock on the door heralded the arrival of Father Pascal and a neatly dressed and solemn gentleman. The three Frenchmen held a whispered conversation after which the Abbé came over with the new arrival.

'My friend here is a doctor. He looks at your back.'

A brief examination and some painful pressings followed by breathing by numbers directed by the Abbé culminated in a swift diagnosis.

'There is no break,' translated the Abbé. 'You have a crack,' and diving into his dictionary added: 'Rib!'

I gave up a silent prayer as the doctor began to strap up my lower ribcage with a wide strip of cloth which seemed to be elasticated. 'A week or two,' said the Abbé, you will be good!'

The doctor wasted no time; he was gone in a flash with the briefest of adieus.

'Rest now,' suggested the Abbé. 'Tomorrow you rise early for the workers' train. Father Pascal will guide you.'

I felt cosy and warm and with my new support confidently comfortable. Bidding the Abbé good night, my thanks being waved away by his kindly hands, I followed Father Pascal to another door off the outside corridor. We entered a small room with two wooden bunk beds against one wall. I tried to reach the top one but I wasn't in the right trim yet! Father Pascal placed a restraining hand on my shoulder and pointed to the lower bunk. '*Dormez bien,*' he said as I slipped instantly into the arms of Morpheus.

# CHAPTER FOUR

# To Paris

I was running down a long corridor with the sound of heavy footsteps behind me. The thumps were getting nearer and nearer as I reached the end of the corridor across which was a high rail. I jumped for dear life and jumped straight into consciousness. Father Pascal was shaking my shoulder and quietly rapping the upright of the bunk bed. Handing me my clothes to put on he indicated that I must hurry. Used to acting in emergencies I quickly shot out of bed feeling only a dull ache in my back. To my amazement I realised that my silk long johns, oversocks and shirt had all been laundered. How on earth anyone had managed that in the time available I had no idea, but following the previous night's bath, fresh underwear made life extremely bearable, I felt like a king! Nothing had been done to my outer garments because I had explained to the Abbé that I was sure that their unkempt appearance had saved me from inquisitiveness.

I tried putting on my own long johns and trousers and found that I could cope pretty well by lying on my back on the bunk and lifting my legs slightly. Bending the knees seemed to be much more possible than yesterday and I rolled back off the bunk to complete the operation. Father Pascal nodded in appreciation, and again signalled for me to make haste; holding out to me a pair of serviceable brown boots. They pinched a bit but at least they were a vast improvement on the shoes I had arrived in; however much I was grateful for them. Pulling on the battledress jacket I followed Father Pascal from the room, yawning and easing a bit of stiffness out of my bones. The corridor outside was filled with the tantalising smell of coffee and hot bread.

The Abbé was up and already sitting at a low table set for three. As we entered his room he rose and waved his arms towards the table: 'I hope you sleep well,' he said. 'We must eat now.'

We tucked into hot rolls and coffee and some nondescript jam, followed by some cheese and grapes. I could have eaten the food for all three of us quite easily but it was no time to appear ravenous and I curbed my impulse eating carefully every crumb placed before me.

As soon as we had finished, the Abbé began again. 'Now,' he said, 'we have food for you in here', lifting up a cardboard box tied with string. 'All the workmen use them and you look the same.' He rummaged again behind him and produced a flat bottle 'Cold coffee,' he explained, 'for your *pantalons*', pointing at my trouser pocket. 'Now. You go to Gare de l'Est from St Dizier. You must have a return ticket.' Another look in his dictionary. 'Understand? Father Pascal will go with you to the station.'

I nodded and looked at my chronometer, just after 4 a.m., or maybe 5 a.m. in this part of France. The Abbé smiled back. 'Now, go,' he commanded. 'God be with you.'

We all stood up and without thinking I grabbed the Abbé by the shoulders and kissed him on both cheeks as I had seen Frenchmen do. His face was rough-shaven and as I released him there was the suspicion of a tear. Had I stayed any longer there would have been one in my eye, but turning quickly I followed Father Pascal out of the room without looking back.

Clutching my parcel, I negotiated the many doors and staircases that it took before we emerged from a side door of the church into an area unfamiliar and quite dark. The swish of Father Pascal's robe was all I had to go by at times, but more often than not his white face was within a pace or two. Ducking down a number of streets, presumably to avoid as many citizens of an awakening town as possible, we came to a large open space fringed with trees. At the far side there were a number of lights and vehicles were moving in both directions.

Father Pascal pointed to the lights and nodded. The station, no less. He placed his hand on my chest, silently asking me to stay still beside a tree and went off to check that the train was running, as the Abbé had arranged. The feeling of being exposed began to rise again inside me in this murky square after several minutes and I was starting to make alternative plans in my mind when Father Pascal appeared again. He grabbed my hands and nodded.

'*Aller et retour*,' he said, reminding me that I was to ask for a return ticket. '*Au revoir*,' he added smiling, and we hugged and kissed cheeks like brothers.

Father Pascal slipped into the darkness soon afterwards, but I am certain in my own mind that he stayed near that station until the train pulled out. With butterflies in my stomach I approached my severest test so far. Breathing in the night air in a deep gulp I set off across the remainder of the open space and crossed the road into the station. A queue of figures lining up before an open window quickly pinpointed the ticket office for me and I joined the end pretending to be bored with events. Others joined the queue behind me and I felt safer in my position, keeping an eye out as to what was taking place ahead in the line.

The Abbé had told me what the fare would be, but I would call less attention to myself if I acted in much the same fashion as the other workers. None of the travellers from what I could see had used any high value bank notes and I quickly got together enough small notes from my escape money to cover the cost of the ticket.

The man immediately in front of me shoved his notes under the ticket office grille, grunting, '*Paris.*'

An indistinguishable mumble came from inside the ticket office and the man said, '*Oui.*' Out came his ticket and I moved up into his place pushing my notes under the grille. The ticket office clerk looked up at me.

'*Paris,*' I said in a low growl.

He looked at me and asked, '*Aller ou aller et retour?*'

I kept a straight face as I growled, '*Aller et retour*', wondering what question had been asked the man who had just said, '*Oui.*' Perhaps the ticket office clerk knew him and that he always took a return ticket. It nearly threw me, but I had come through all right because there was the ticket in front of me. Taking it casually, I moved to the left following the other passengers and hurried up to catch the man in front so that there would be no embarrassing gap in the queue which might provoke a question from the ticket collector. Under the lamp light we were just dim faceless figures and we all went through with the collector waving us impatiently on to the long windswept platform smelling deliciously of all the aromas one connects with steam engines and railways.

People were forming into small groups, volubly exchanging the latest tittle-tattle, and probably complaining about the poor time keeping of the trains. All I had to do was to get on the train when it arrived; there could be no mistakes, the only train at this time was going to Paris. A stone pillar supporting the roof of the station offered a darkened recess at the side of it so I ambled along towards a point opposite it and then, as if as an afterthought, moved over to the recess and laid my back against the wall.

I was out of the way here but could see all that was going on. Some German soldiers came on to the platform in full kit, possibly going on leave to Paris or somewhere. They placed their packs in a neat pile and stood around loudly guffawing and passing remarks, amusing only to themselves. The workers paid no attention to them, but it was noticeable that the earlier gaiety of the Frenchmen had disappeared, and they were staring stolidly ahead of them, in anguish most likely. I felt an overwhelming sadness at their resignation.

Time went by as it does on stations throughout the world and first light was beginning to show on the horizon. The Germans had quietened down but stood kicking their high boots together as the cool wind swept the platform. I shuddered behind my pillar but I wasn't making any move until that train came in. And suddenly there it was jangling and clanking into the station, giving off jets of steam against the waiting throng lining the platform. I moved across quickly to push into a front position as I had often done in the tube in London.

The carriages juddered to a halt and immediately in front of me was a door labelled, '*Nur für Wehrmacht.*' Great! I thought, not for the army. At least it will be one of the carriages free from German Servicemen. Later I was to learn that it meant 'Only for the Wehrmacht'!

I opened the door quickly and lifted myself aboard. Still clutching my food box I managed to get a few yards along the corridor when I was halted quite roughly by restraining hands on my shoulder. Looking round in half anger expecting to see other workers trying to get to a seat before me, I found that I was being collared by the very German soldiers who had been on the platform in front of me. There were loud cries sounding like, '*Franzosisch Dummkopf*' and '*Raus*' as I was passed like some rag doll from one soldier to another along the corridor, and finally pushed out of the door by the last one to a chorus of taunting laughter.

Pulling myself together I got up from where I was laid sprawled on the platform and went a little further down where I would see ordinary civilians in an open carriage without compartments. One corner seat had not been filled so I got in attracting no comment from my neighbours and sat down collecting myself with my eyes closed. Perhaps the best thing to do would be to feign sleep most of the way. As it happened, most people were nodding off, even small children whom I was surprised to see at that time in the morning.

The sun came up as we passed through several small towns stopping at most of them. More and more travellers were getting on and the carriage was uncomfortably full with people standing in every available space. For my part I welcomed the crush, it gave me an ideal excuse for not taking part in any conversation and it meant that the press of people at the ticket barrier at the Gare de l'Est would be more than the ticket collectors could manage.

The journey wore on and I surreptitiously slipped the last piece of fortified chocolate into my mouth, it might be a while before I could take advantage of the Abbé's food box. Another doze and I came to, to find the train slowing down as it entered the first suburbs of Paris. My plan by then was to head for Montparnasse on the other side of the Seine, sufficiently out of the way of the administrative centre of Paris and with a reputation for being friendly to foreigners. I had certainly found it so when I visited it during the phoney war of 1940.

The other passengers were beginning to get their boxes and bundles together, indicating that we hadn't far to go. I rubbed away part of the condensation on the side window and saw the beginnings of a station approach, multiple rails, bands of workmen and small engines shunting back and forth. I decided to get out as soon as the last standing passengers had made an exit. In this way I would be in the middle of a noisy throng. A series of jerks and clatters and we were under the canopy of the Gare de l'Est, running at last to a gentle stop alongside the platform. Doors burst open, banging against the side of the carriage and the stampede began. I pulled myself up by the luggage rack and realised again how stiff I was in the joints. Putting this at the back of my mind, I moved to the door and was good-naturedly jostled onto the platform.

A sea of figures stretched before me and I had to keep up with the fast pace of my neighbours. Nearing the ticket barrier I could see odd groups of people waiting for arriving passengers, and, the occasional single figure staring at the press of people which to me had a far more sinister overtone. I pushed in amongst a bunch of men wearing greasy blue overalls and waited my turn to go through the barrier. As luck would have it, another official came to the barrier and opened a further portion of it to reduce the mounting pressure of people wanting to get through. In the end I went through half hiding myself behind the backs of the workers around me, without offering my ticket at all. Like a pebble washed up on the seashore I was well inside the station foyer before the rush subsided, and then suddenly I was on my own again with more than one exit to choose from. The majority of the workmen were heading out of the largest exit so I did the same, once again feeling that safety lay in acting as if one was familiar with the routine of daily travel.

I wasn't ready, however, for the blinding light of day after coming out of the semi-darkness of the station foyer. Standing on the pavement of the Rue Lafayette I screwed up my eyeballs, trying to familiarise myself with the constantly moving scene before me and the overpowering sounds of a big city noisily coming to life in the turmoil of traffic and street cries. One thing was certain, I couldn't stay gawping any longer! A quick glance at the sun gave me a rough bearing and I turned left heading west into the city centre, limping slightly again as my feet hit the hard pavement and sent a rippling ache through my side. The Rue Lafayette seemed interminable and already large numbers of people including all manner of German servicemen were on the move walking to wherever their place of work or duty was situated. I was starting to feel uncomfortable, walking, as it felt, against the stream and I resolved to get off the busier streets as much as possible. My destination was at first the Eiffel Tower, easy to find and guiding me to the area where I felt help would be forthcoming, but I knew that I had a good distance to go yet. A main crossroads forced my hand and I turned to the right along a less crowded thoroughfare. Feeling a little tired I kept an eye out for a church which I could enter and rest in for a while. Minutes passed and the canyon of buildings seemed to stretch for ever but much like a mirage the buildings slowly gave way to reveal an open space, in fact quite a large area from which several streets radiated.

In the centre stood an imposing church, high towered like a cathedral with a huge wooden door open as if beckoning people to mount the stone steps to worship. I increased my pace and slithered inside like a homing reptile. The inside seemed vast and a number of pews contained people in silent prayer. Crossing myself I flopped quietly into a side pew to ponder upon my next step. To my left I could see a row of confessionals with low doors and heavy blue curtains: now and then one of the silent figures in front of me would rise and disappear behind the folds of curtain. I began to form an idea in my mind that this might be the way of getting assistance, Montparnasse was a long way off and I could save myself a great deal of trouble and exposure to danger. The bulk of the flat bottle in my trousers pocket reminded me that I was thirsty and I had a quick sip of the cold coffee despite the picture it must have given to anyone watching me!

Mentally emboldened I rose, and making my way with head slightly bowed, I reached the first confessional box and swinging back the low door passed through the curtains into the semi-darkness within. I was looking for a bell or some means of attracting attention when a small trap opened in the wooden wall dividing me from the priest. A low stool was in place underneath the aperture and I lowered myself onto it, waiting for some kind of request. Having no idea of the procedure and whether some opening remark or prayer was required from me, I gently coughed and awaited events. A soft low voice came through the aperture obviously enquiring about my reason for being there, and, standing up, I could make out the priest's face. I spoke my phrases parrot-fashion once more and I could see his surprise that an RAF flyer had managed to get to Paris looking for help. He was very distant in his manner and in some strange way he aroused my suspicion, I didn't like the situation I was in, especially when he made a reference to '*L'Ambassade Britannique*'. '*Restez là*,' the priest finally said and disappeared from sight out of a back door. Feeling that I was a sitting duck inside the confessional box I was in no mood to take chances. As I stepped out through the curtains I remembered with alarm that my food box was underneath the pew that I had first sat in, so I hurriedly retrieved it and edged round the inside perimeter of the church heading for a smaller door at the far end which was also open; sunbeams lighting up the wooden tops of the pews.

From the open doorway you could see most of what was going on in the square outside so I took up a position just behind the door facing inwards to the church. This had the advantage of making me look as if I were interested in the architecture whilst I could keep an eye on the confessional box and also from time to time look out for any new arrivals appearing in the square and making for the church itself. Several minutes passed but there was no activity around the confessionals other than the occasional worshipper entering for confession. Something inside me was warning me to keep on my toes and on my next peep outside I saw a large open car drawing up at the far end of the church and two men in long raincoats and soft hats getting out. It was too much of a coincidence. I had no idea whether my priest would return, and what if he had phoned for the security police? My warning voice won me over; there was plenty of Paris to explore yet and this was not quite the place to be. Quickly I stepped out into the sunlight and took off for the road exactly opposite; any road would do for the moment but I managed a rueful smile as I saw its name 'Rue de Londres'.

Hurrying along to put some distance between myself and the church I took some left and right turns through small streets, encountering small cafés and shops selling all manner of things, quite a few passers-by who appeared oblivious to my presence and even the occasional gendarme who though curious for a brief second gave no sign of greater interest. I felt a little safer but needed to be off the streets for a while in case anyone was looking for me. Turning into a larger street I saw several billboards ahead of me and the frontage of a cinema advertising its films for the day. Why not, I thought. This would give me at least three hours of rest and refuge and I would be off the streets at the busiest time; by the look of the sun it was not yet noon. My greatest mistake so far was to forget to keep my chronometer wound up and I was having to rely on my wits for time until I could find a public clock. Outside the cinema I stood for a while looking at the stills displayed, purely to give me the air of an habitué of the area. Then, slowly and deliberately I mounted the pseudo marble steps, took my largest bank note out of my pocket offered it at the ticket window and waited for some sort of question about which seat I wanted. On my last visit to Paris in 1940 I had attended theatres and cinemas and had always asked for 'Fauteuils' or stalls. I was ready with that but as it happened nothing was necessary. The lady behind the grille gave me a ticket and some change and I turned to the entrance door in some puzzlement thinking that maybe at this time of day there was one fixed price for upstairs and downstairs. Another elderly lady took my ticket and shepherded me to a seat near the back of the cinema and it then became clear to me why I had not been asked about seating. The cinema consisted of one floor only.

Thankful that another tricky situation had not materialised I settled back to watch a film about Emile Brazza, the founder of the town of Brazzaville in the Congo, and another about a love triangle in rural France, interspersed by a newsreel mostly German in origin. The plot and the language were mostly beyond me, but I was comfortable and resting. During the newsreel which was unaccountably noisy I managed to get into the food box and eat some of the bread and cheese and take a further swig from the bottle of coffee. The film about Brazza had come round again, and some of the scenes began to look familiar and I realised that the cinema programme was continuous without any breaks at the end of each performance. Making my way to the exit I nodded to the elderly usherette, crossed the foyer and once again blinked on reaching the sunlit street outside.

There were fewer people about than when I went in and my side of the street was in partial shadow. This was to my advantage and I kept inconspicuously to the side as I turned left to head west once more. Passers-by were noticeably unsmiling and I saw as if for the first time that the colour and gaiety that had personified Paris in 1940 had been replaced by drabness and sullen resignation. It seemed a sad reflection on the French people as a whole. I had known many extrovert and brave French servicemen and I hoped that I would be able to contact some of them who would certainly be carrying on clandestine activities against the occupying Germans. As it was, no one paid the slightest attention as I limped along apart from one lady dressed in some black shiny material who gave my scratched face a long look, and with eyes filled with compassion raised her hand momentarily to her lips and passed on. I stopped at the next shop window to look at myself, the battered flat cap atop a white face with its diagonal cuts, the well worn battledress and baggy trousers and large country boots. Truly a candidate for a Hal Roach comedy, but at least I was an acceptable sight in that part of Paris.

The road seemed exceptionally long and the dull pain restarted in my side, and the tight boots were beginning to make themselves felt. I hadn't really had a decent night's sleep since coming down and once again I began to feel very tired indeed. The cinema had been an ideal shelter but I had not been able to nod off during the films for fear of what might develop. There was no two ways about it, I needed a sleep soon. Another large road junction provided the answer, as from there I could see the upper part of the Eiffel Tower. Bearing left I made towards it, although it was still quite some way away. After a while the road began to run alongside a large open park, bristling with trees and bushes. Leaving the road, I turned up a short side track onto sweet-smelling grass under trees still holding some leaves. Large shrubs encircled the spot and the prospect of a rest under one of them out of sight of the world was too much to pass up. I sank to the ground and rolled under the nearest shrub having branches down to the ground. Inside was a cool cavern, a little breezy but inviting and quiet. The foodbox and cap made a makeshift pillow and I drifted off like a dormouse.

The sound of children's voices broke my reverie and I awoke with bits of dried leaves in my mouth. Sitting up hastily I peered through the shrub and saw that it was bordering a large sloping field in which several children were engaged in the international game of chase. I gathered up my cap and box and rolled out the other side. The sun was moving across the sky now and it looked to be well into the afternoon. En route once more having brushed myself as much as possible I began looking for somewhere to stop and eat the contents of the foodbox. The park was still bordering the road I was on and some way along I noticed a wooden seat alongside the perimeter path of the park and looking out towards a small bandstand. There was no one about so I hopped over to the seat and spread my food.

The Abbé had given me a simple meal of bread, cheese, grapes and an onion, but it was a superb meal at that very moment and the view was enchanting with a backdrop of wooded rises, ponds and glades. Munching away, half musing I caught the sound of footsteps in the distance and turned to see a body of German soldiers making their way along the perimeter path. They looked terribly like a patrol and the remains of my last mouthful of food took a long time to swallow as the soldiers got nearer. Flight was impossible, so once again I would have to rely on brazening it out and I leant back against the seat with arms outstretched along the top bar. The soldiers were getting near enough to see each face quite clearly, when they were abruptly brought to a halt. With some relief I noticed that they were not carrying rifles but the last two men were pulling a handcart. A smart left turn and they all broke off towards the bandstand and began setting up for a concert. The ludicrousness of the situation appealed to my sense of humour, but it was not discreet to stay around too long and after listening to a few short warming up pieces, I got up and resumed my travels.

The Eiffel Tower was over to my left now and I walked a great number of streets keeping it mostly ahead of me. Walking became an automatic action, I was not retaining any idea of where I had been, my sole endeavour was to keep moving. My next turn led me into a much larger and busier avenue, the buildings grew a little higher and I lost sight of my landmark temporarily. A little frustrated perhaps I hurried along and all at once burst in upon the most familiar French sight of all, the Place d'Etoile with the Arc de Triomphe in the centre.

Oncoming signs of exhaustion dictated that I should move from there over the other side of the river as quickly as possible, and the Avenue Marceau was soon under my feet although it seemed to stretch endlessly. But, in time, there I was crossing the Seine over the Pont d'Alma, hardly taking in the magnificent sights around me. I had become an automaton, and later passing by the Eiffel Tower never gave it a glance as I headed towards Montparnasse with unconscious determination. The light seemed to be fading a bit and a small maggot of doubt entered my mind; was I going to find a resting place before dark? I tried a few more left turns and right turns and lo and behold, as if in answer to my doubts, or was it a prayer, I walked into the Square de Felix Fauré and saw the little church in its centre.

I stood and looked at it and hung my head for a moment. There was little point in going on. This was where I was going to have to trust to luck. The door of the church was closed but not locked and I raised the latch and quietly entered. There was quite a lot of candlelight inside and I looked back at the sky through the door and realised that it was deepening and heralding evening. I decided to search for a priest and walked the length of the church without success. Someone came through the main door, prompting me to sit in the front pew and wait. I bent myself as if in prayer and kept my eyes half open so that I could see what was happening. My throat was dry but I put that at the back of my mind, the empty coffee bottle and foodbox were sitting under the bench in front of the park bandstand.

The person who had entered the church came slowly and reverently to a statue by the side of the altar rail, already surrounded by numerous candles, and lit another one. It was a youngish woman in black but she gave me no glance. She curtsied and went to a pew a little further back. The silence and peace which pervaded the building, the flickering candles and smell of stale incense began to affect my mind and, as if in a haze, I felt an overpowering desire to relax and rest. The mental picture of the inside of the church slipped away and I disappeared into a dark void.

# CHAPTER FIVE

# In Paris

A gentle rocking roused me from my slumber and I awoke with a start to find a priest bending over me obviously concerned. He asked a gentle question which was too indistinct for me to catch and I launched into my parrot phrases once more. Hardly had the first phrase finished before he placed his hand momentarily over my mouth. Helping me up by the armpits he motioned for me to follow him towards a side door.

In the candlelight I could see that he was an elderly man, short and stocky, his biretta and cassock had seen better days, but the face below it was kind and sympathetic. We passed through a side door crossed a narrow corridor and entered a small vestry. He closed the door slipping the bolt and turned to me and said:

'Good evening, my son. I am Abbé Dufour. Please sit down and rest.' His English had a very thick French accent but how enjoyable it was to hear it! 'You must be very tired and hungry and thirsty and we will see to that in a moment but first you must tell me how you came here.'

Leaning back in a soft chair at my ease I had no difficulty in pouring out the story of my adventures thus far and Abbé Dufour listened with grave attentiveness. Occasionally he would stop me for an explanation in more simple terms, but his English was overall very comprehensive and I felt more and more as if I was being gently interrogated. He was amused at the bandstand incident and asked to see the remainder of the escape money I had been supplied with, satisfying himself that it was genuine. My story over, he took a look at the scratches on my face, touched me on the knee and said, 'Wait here a little while.' He turned back at the door to give me one further searching look and with a swish of his cassock was gone.

I sat there for what seemed some considerable time wondering whether I was any better off than when I had felt trapped in the confessional box. At least the door bolt was on my side. But more reasonable thoughts came flooding in and I began to assess the Abbé as a trustworthy person and much more likely to help me than the last priest. A bump on the door startled me and brought my preoccupation to an end. Abbé Dufour came in backwards bearing a tray having used his posterior to flip the latch. Meaty smells rose from a blue bowl on the tray and beside the bowl lay a large hunk of dark brown bread and a breakfast cup of coffee.

Smiling as he placed the tray on the vestry table the Abbé waved his hand towards it saying: 'Help yourself. I will be back later with some friends of mine.' He noticed my questioning frown, and added, 'It's all right. They are not police.' Reassuringly he put his hand on my shoulder and left the room quickly.

Well, I thought to myself, this is where my solo effort ends. If the Abbé can come up with some contacts, I may be able to get back to England somehow. Mentally basking in optimistic sunlight I savoured every bit of the soup, bread and coffee. Back in the soft chair I lay back and awaited events. I hadn't long to wait, hardly having time to gaze around the room at the pictures of priests of various ages and the religious paraphernalia that was all about. The Abbé came back in, followed by two swarthy civilians wearing dark hats and raincoats. A wave of apprehension went through me; these men were not unlike the two I had seen at the last church.

Coming forward smiling the Abbé introduced his companions as Jules and Marcel, members of an organisation who might be able to help me. They both shook hands with me and quickly sat at the table, one producing a writing pad. The Abbé took a chair by me, presumably for my reassurance. After a brief silence during which they both studied me intensely, they began to ask questions alternately in halting English. The first few were about the details of the raid I had been on, where my base was, squadron, aircraft, crew etc, to which I merely gave my number rank and name.

They were clearly disconcerted by my refusal to divulge operational information, and changed tack to ask where I was born. Hearing that I was a Londoner, they brightened up considerably and launched into a series of questions about the sights of the city and where they were situated. Then about my family and names back to my grandparents, and suddenly two questions about general Air Force practice, the first requesting the name of the aircrew magazine and the second asking for the composition of the post-op aircrew breakfast. Both men seemed to be happy with the replies, nodding to each other in confirmation each time and I imagined that the questioning was over. Not a bit of it, we went on to some simple questions about cricket, the various kinds of English coins and finally newspapers.

This seemed to do it and the men passed a brief comment in French between themselves and the Abbé who turned to me and said, 'They are quite satisfied and will help you now. They must be very careful not to accept enemy infiltrators.' I breathed a silent sigh of relief because both of the men looked quite capable of dispatching anyone without turning a hair.

A further lively conversation took place between the men and the Abbé and at the end of it the men nodded their goodbyes and swiftly left. 'They are arranging for you to pass the night in a safe place,' the Abbé explained. 'Later you will go to another place outside Paris which will be even safer for a few days.' He opened a small cabinet and took out some small glasses and a bottle. 'A little cognac,' he smiled, 'to celebrate your falling amongst friends.' Sitting comfortably in the soft chair I could feel the warmth of the cognac permeating my body, and for the first time in ages I abandoned myself in total relaxation. 'We must get you something for your face and have your back looked at,' continued the Abbé. 'You will be well cared for now and you will be able to rest and return quickly to full health.'

'Can they get me back to England?' I asked.

'We shall see. We shall see,' the Abbé whispered. 'You must leave everything to them.'

The cognac and the friendly atmosphere loosened my tongue a little and I was enjoying the opportunity to chat with my host. He took no advantage of that to pry into any operational details but we talked mostly about my previous visit to France with the Advanced Air Striking Force. The tales of outnumbered and obsolete aircraft and the ignominious final retreat made him shake his head sadly. Like most Frenchmen he could not understand how the collapse had happened so quickly when the defending French and British armies had been so strong in numbers. He was well informed about the Battle of Britain and the later efforts of the Allies, curiously so, for a simple parish priest.

A knock on the door punctuated our conversation and the Abbé called '*Entrez.*'

A young woman came in slowly carrying a large paper bag. She was dressed in black which accentuated her pale olive-shaped face and as she came forward, after a brief curtsey to the Abbé, I could see that she was showing the same signs of life under the occupation of the Germans as the people I had noticed in the streets. A sadness clouded her face which was pinched with undernourishment. She looked much older as she moved into full light and exchanged words with the Abbé.

He held her hand for a moment and then introduced her. 'This is Marguerite who will shelter you in her parents' flat for the night or perhaps two. Your uniform is far too dangerous to wear in the city so she has brought you some other clothes.' She shook my hand very nervously and with a wan smile handed me the paper bag. It contained a fairly old brown jacket with a built up left shoulder as if it had been made for a hunchback, and a nondescript pair of black and white striped trousers. A rough grey shirt and sleeveless pullover completed the ensemble. I remember thinking to myself that with my scratched face and slight limp I would be a good prospect for one of Lon Chaney's films wearing this particular outfit. Still, I supposed that garments were at a premium and I would not look out of place in the general crowd.

The Abbé discreetly led Marguerite out of the room whilst I exchanged my clothing. Parting with my faithful old battledress was a bit of a wrench, and I wondered whether if I happened to be captured, I could be treated as a spy in civilian clothes and possibly shot. My identity discs hung reassuringly round my neck but this would be no guarantee that I was a bona fide flyer. This was not the time for pessimism, however, and I did a turn of the room to get used to my new attire. My reflection in the glass of some of the lower pictures hanging on the wall suggested a reasonable appearance and I began to feel happier about the disguise. There was a moment of embarrassment when I was caught adjusting my cap at a rakish angle by the Abbé who had silently entered the room to see if I had finished dressing. I snatched the cap off my head like a frightened schoolboy and the Abbé burst out laughing.

'Come my friend,' he said. 'You need a good night's sleep. You could look worse, you know.'

Marguerite was waiting in the corridor as we both stepped out and the Abbé led us to a side door with a hand on each of our shoulders. It was quite dark outside but there were a number of lights in the buildings surrounding the Square, which surprised me greatly until I realised that it was hardly likely that the city of Paris would be bombed by the British. There was no time for protracted goodbyes and the pair of us melted into the gloom with the briefest of handshakes and *mercis*. The Square itself was very quiet but as we turned into a main thoroughfare from one of the side streets we were

**Above** A further picture of the NCOs of the crew, taken in the sergeants' mess, Binbrook, in early 1941. Left to right: Peter Tracey, myself, Doug Preston, George Jolley and Paddy Taylor.

**Right** Squadron Leader Sidney Horace Fox DFM (*Chris Ailsby Historical Collection*).

**Above** The graves of the crew at the cemetery of Nant-le-Grand, near Ligny-en-Barrois.

**Left** Emmeline Troclet as a young woman.

soon caught up in a jostling throng of people, mostly German servicemen with their girlfriends on their way to a night's entertainment at a café or *boîte*.

I felt Marguerite's arm slip behind mine as she endeavoured to make it look as if we were more than passing strollers, and I mentally gave her full marks for her astuteness. She was by no means timorous, and as we looked at each other and smiled I could see that her face had lost its sadness and had gained a certain air of defiance as if she was enjoying the moment of deception in front of the Germans. She hurried me along for a hundred yards or so and then pulled me into an entry between two shops. Next to one of the shop doors was a larger and more substantial one which she opened to give us entry into a small dimly lit hall with numbered doors leading off. A staircase with faded brown carpet led to upper rooms and we climbed two floors in silence to reach No 37, Marguerite's parents' flat.

She threw the door back hastily, pointing for me to go in and then followed me, turning to slip bolts on both the top and bottom of the door. Obviously taking no chances. The flat was divided by a wide central hall, and she led me through the first door on the left into a largish salon half filled with old fashioned wooden furniture with blue leather upholstery. Glass cabinets lined the walls displaying china and ornaments of various kinds. A tall grandfather clock ticked off the hours. It was a well lived in room and carried the subtle odours of years of cleaning and polishing.

'Sit please,' ordered Marguerite surprisingly.

'You speak English then,' I exclaimed.

'Little only,' came the answer. 'Better you speak French,' she smiled.

She disappeared for a while and came back carrying two cups of black bitter coffee, and some thick striped pyjamas. We sipped in silence, occasionally smiling at each other, neither of us wanting to start a conversation which we couldn't keep up.

'*Voilà*,' she said eventually, draining her cup. '*Venez avec moi.*'

I had emptied my cup long ago, and drowsiness was beginning to take hold of me again. As I followed her from the room she turned and handed me the pyjamas and pointed across the hall to a room opposite. This was obviously a kitchen-cum-dining room, again furnished in well worn genteel fashion. Along one wall, under a large photo portrait of a well fed married couple, was a made-up camp bed which sported a huge eiderdown covered in a fleur de lys pattern. Marguerite pulled back the top sheet, smiled shyly and wished me, '*Dormez bien*'.

As she went out, I remember thinking that she was extremely brave taking me into her flat without a great deal of assurance that I wouldn't do her any harm or try to force myself upon her. I reflected though on the fact that if I had tried to do so my life would have been a little more at risk than it was at that moment. The thought of being pursued by her friends who had questioned me was chilling to say the least and I made a mental pledge to be a good boy at all times. As I undressed, I noticed a framed diploma on the opposite wall which was obviously Marguerite's issued in 1928 with the information '*Née 1906.*' So she was 36 and also a spinster judging by her ringless hand. Brave soul, I thought again, as I slipped between the fresh smelling sheets; things aren't looking so bad after all.

Morning came too quickly though and I woke to find Marguerite anxiously pushing my nearest shoulder. She explained that there was something to eat and drink on the kitchen table and that she had to go to work and would be back at midday. I grunted and nodded that I understood and as she slipped out of the door she turned and put her finger to her mouth. I nodded again; the one thing I was not going to do was to prejudice her safety by advertising my presence in the flat during her absence. Lying quietly musing on what I should do, I came up with the quick and obvious answer. This was my first opportunity for an extended rest for some time, so, after I had washed and had breakfast, I would just stay prone and gather strength. There was plenty of waiting time to come and I would fill that by learning as much of the French language as I could. It was possible to move about the country and the more phrases I picked up the less likely I would be to show surprise or consternation if anyone shot a question at me.

Rolling out of bed on my right side produced a twinge of pain but it didn't last and I stood up feeling much better. Marguerite had left a light on and I made my way carefully over to the table, laid out with coffee pot, rolls and some kind of jam. A smile crossed my face as I saw next to the cup a shaving kit, soap and towel. A large bowl and a jug of warmish water completed the assorted articles. Again she had shown remarkable astuteness, there would be no noise from the plumbing to alert any suspicions. Shaving up to the diagonal cuts on my face would be a bit tricky but I had all the time in the world. Breakfast was delicious but again the coffee was very bitter, perhaps it was the German coffee substitute 'ersatz'. I made a mental note to get some real coffee for her if I could.

Leaving the dirty crockery where it was, I washed in the bowl and then shaved gingerly using a small mirror over the sink. The thought did cross my mind that a clean shaven face might not go with the rest of my get-up, but the delight of having a shave far outweighed any doubts I had. I consoled myself with the fact that I hadn't cleaned my teeth for three days which would add to the shabbiness of my appearance and keep people at their distance. Giving myself a broad yellow smile in the mirror I went back to the bed to await Marguerite's return.

She gave the door of the flat a bit of a thump as she shut it and I came out of a shallow snooze instantly. Entering the kitchen door she seemed in a rush and was surprised to see me still in bed.

'Rise!' she said. 'We must have lunch,' and straightaway started cooking preparations.

I felt no embarrassment in dressing whilst she was cooking as I was well covered up in my long-johns. In any case she was far too busy to gawp at me and I hurried into my clothes and busied myself putting the bedclothes in order. I asked her what time it was and she called out that the clock in the salon kept good time, so I went in and put my chronometer right with French time. It was just after twelve o'clock. An old newspaper lay to the right of the hearth and I picked it up leafing through it idly whilst waiting a further call about lunch. There was something about Rommel and some local news and I was quite pleased to be able to pick out odd words and roughly decipher meanings.

'Monsieur', called Marguerite, 'come now.' Back in the kitchen, full of savoury smells, two bowls of soup were set on the table with a hunk of bread against each. We sat opposite each other exchanging smiles and glances, and quickly despatched the bread and soup.

I eventually broke the silence. 'My name is Herbert, please call me that.'

She nodded and stood up to bring the next course. This turned out to be some wafer thin slices of meat and two large potatoes, and some more bread. 'I go again soon,' she explained, 'but first doctor come at one hour.'

I congratulated her on her English and thanked her. We washed the meal down with water then had cups of that same bitter coffee.

At precisely one o'clock the door bell whirred and a small dapper man with brilliantined hair slid into the apartment. He motioned to me to take off my upper garments and in a very quick professional and workmanlike manner removed the elasticated cloth around my ribs and gave me a thorough examination. Nodding from time to time, he had no need to ask in what areas did I feel any pain, my face gave him an instant answer. He did not seem too anxious about the cuts on my face but treated them with an antiseptic of some kind. Later he produced a thicker piece of elasticated material and strapped up my ribs once more. Satisfied, he had a short word with Marguerite, left a small bottle of the antiseptic lotion, bowed solemnly to me and disappeared as quietly as he came.

Marguerite came back from the apartment door smiling. 'You are not bad!' she said reassuringly. 'You rest a week.' She put on her hat and coat saying, 'Back at five hour. *Au revoir*,' and was gone as swiftly as the doctor. I washed the crockery as best as I could and went back to bed.

The sound of a key in a lock brought me upright in an instant. I could hear Marguerite talking and also male voices which alarmed me for a moment until I realised that the voices were low and not strident or demanding. She entered the kitchen with two young men, thick set six footers and rugged. Unlike the general public they looked extremely fit. Introducing them as 'Jacques', the saturnine curly-haired one with strong white teeth, and 'Maurice', quite blond with a boxer's nose, Marguerite explained, using both French and English, that they were both demobilised Army men from the Chasseurs d'Alpin, the French ski troops. Jacques' father owned a wine shop in the Vincennes area and I was to go there for a few days. Whilst I finished dressing Marguerite prepared some coffee and when we had somewhat silently finished our cups she treated my cuts with the lotion, tucked the bottle into my jacket pocket and gently escorted me to the apartment door where Jacques and Maurice were waiting. A smile reminiscent of the Mona Lisa came over her face.

'*Bon voyage*,' she whispered.

We emerged into the harsh sounds of daytime Paris and walked briskly to the nearby Metro station. I felt conspicuous limping along between the two lofty guardians of my immediate future but no one gave us a second glance. In fact during the whole journey which needed a couple of train rides and a bus, neither the local people nor the occupying troops showed the slightest interest, a fact which steadily increased my confidence. No verbal directions were necessary, I merely went everywhere as the filling in the sandwich, with Jacques and occasionally Maurice leading. After a bewildering assortment of streets and open spaces, alleys and side turnings we reached Jacques father's shop. All part of making sure we were not being followed I suppose; it was really sound common sense. A last glance up and down the street by Maurice who nodded to Jacques and we entered the shop door and went straight through the rows of bottles, through the raised mahogany counter and up some carpeted stairs into the living quarters above. The salon, or lounge, was long and roomy, very modern and sprinkled liberally with soft chairs and sofas.

Jacques' parents were already there, a slim, tall, grey-bearded man with a ruddy face and quick friendly eyes and a more petite lady very smartly dressed, large almond eyes and high cheekbones with dark hair swept backwards into a bun. They made a great fuss of me and in a trice came glasses of wine and sweetmeats. Communication was proving a little difficult for neither Jacques nor Maurice had a handful of English words between them and his parents none at all. We managed, supported by the French words I had collected on my travels which were ever a source of laughter to them when used in my explanations.

Eventually I was invited to see the guest room where I was to stay. It looked eminently suitable for a young girl, a high bed with a coverlet filled with a mass of embroidery, soft pink carpeting and ornaments galore, and everywhere frills on furniture and windows. A little different to what I had been used to but I thanked my hosts profusely. Jacques showed me the bathroom and flung a dressing gown and bath towel on the bed and I was left to make myself presentable before the evening meal. The strapping round my ribs was easy to remove and I made a neat pile of my clothing before wrapping the dressing gown around me. The bathroom, like the lounge, was sumptuous and the sunken bath and other furnishings all of light blue were of a high quality. I felt reluctant to make a mess.

The sheer joy of having a luxurious bath finally over came any scruples I may have had and I ran the bath with relish. Soon I was deep in a perfumed sea of suds, occasionally waving at myself in the mirrored tiles across the room, and singing snatches from a Bing Crosby repertoire. It was superb, and I stayed immersed for what seemed for ever, but like all good things, it had to end. Jacques stuck his head round the bathroom door and smiled.

'Eat soon,' he said and disappeared.

Back in the bedroom I found that my pile of clothes had vanished and across the bed lay socks, underwear, a check shirt and trousers, a new pullover and a pair of soft moccasin slippers. I shook my head smiling as Jacques walked in. He seemed no stranger to elasticated strapping and I was soon feeling supported in comfort around the midriff. Fully dressed I felt a new man. We went back through the salon to the dining room beyond where Jacques' parents and Maurice were already waiting. The elegant table was beautifully laid out and we spent the next hour or two eating and chatting through several courses accompanied by liberal quantities of various wines. It seemed completely unreal, but eminently enjoyable and I mused on the fact that the family had to be in touch with the black market. Marguerite's circumstances were at the other end of the scale and I sympathised with her from my new nest of creature comforts. The food and wine eventually got to me and I declined coffee and liqueurs, feeling decidedly muzzy and ready for bed. Unsteadily I returned to the bedroom, threw off my clothes and sank into a glorious sleep.

Days passed as I enjoyed ideal luxury. Huge breakfasts and meals and the inevitable wine, cigarettes, magazines, everything was to hand and I had virtually the run of the suite whilst everyone looked after the business. It occurred to me that I was there to recover and restore my strength and I wondered how long the convalescence would last. My French was improving, the cuts on my face were healing well and my ribs felt extremely comfortable. It came as no surprise when Jacques appeared one morning after breakfast to tell me that I was moving again late that afternoon. He would not be coming with me as he and Maurice had another appointment, but another friend called Luc would be my guide. Presenting me with my long johns, freshly laundered, he indicated that I could keep the clothes I was wearing and shrugged aside my fervent thanks. We said goodbye French style and he cuffed my ear affectionately before leaving.

After lunch with Jacques' parents, a cheery affair during which they expressed their confidence that I would be back in England soon, I went back to the bedroom for a siesta, not knowing when I might enjoy again the lap of luxury. A cloth haversack lay on the bed and a short coat made of thick blue cloth. Jacques again, I thought, and then noticed that my boots had also gone, replaced by a stout pair of dark brown walking shoes. They had been worn quite a bit but what a joy they were to wear after the tight prisons my feet had been in since St Dizier. I stuffed my long johns and slippers in the haversack and lay back on the bed ruminating on the kindness of Jacques and his family. It would be a wrench to leave them.

Dusk was approaching when Jacques' father knocked at the bedroom door to announce that Luc had arrived. I grabbed my coat and haversack and made my way to the salon when Jacques' father introduced me to Luc, a short, dark, rat-faced man looking like a typical Hollywood crook. He looked tough enough to look after himself and he was impatient to leave. We were joined by Jacques' mother and after quick goodbyes and an odd tear from Madame, Luc and I went out of the shop as swiftly as I had entered. Outside the street was filled with people and I recognized the hurried scramble for home that one gets in a city rush hour.

It was the ideal time to move about and in my new apparel I was more confident than ever. Bracing my shoulders and with a swift look at my capable guide, I looked forward to more high adventure. My wish was soon gratified, enough to prompt me not to tempt fate again. We had changed trains to board an inner city Metro carriage filled with workers of all sorts and jolted to a halt at one of the stations along the line. Several German Servicemen aggressively pushed their way into the compartment and I found myself strap hanging face to face with two Luftwaffe pilots, one wearing the Iron Cross with oak leaves. They passed the time in idle chatter but one of them was becoming increasingly interested in either the marks on my face, or me myself, and looking quizzically at me as if he recognised me. Luc must have seen all this and as the train decelerated into the next station, he tugged at the base of my coat and we both turned towards the farther door, hurriedly shouldering our way through the other passengers. My heart was in my mouth, and had been since the arrival of the pilots, and I was half expecting a harsh command to stop but we made it to the door and jumped onto the platform into the anonymity of the waiting crowd.

Luc gave me a broad grin, showing broken yellow teeth, and shrugged theatrically. He motioned to a hard bench and we sat and waited for another train. Another short journey followed and eventually I was following Luc up some stairs into the evening air with all the sounds of Paris about us. The shop windows seemed faintly lit but there were plenty of people gazing at the displays which were extremely meagre compared with pre-war Paris, or even pre-Occupied Paris. It was early November but the air was still warm as we made our way swiftly through the throng. Soon we were twisting and turning through side streets until we reached the relative calm of an open square. There was a church in the centre which looked very familiar. Of course! It was the Abbé Dufour's church, but we were not stopping there. In fact we took the self same route that I had taken previously with Marguerite. Five minutes later I knew my destination as we stood in front of the door to her parents' flat.

Marguerite had either just come home in the rush hour or had been told to be home to await unnamed individuals; she was genuinely surprised to see Luc and me. She let us into the flat and immediately went into a private conversation with Luc, who at one point, as if to assure her, showed her an automatic pistol he was carrying. They remained whispering for a while longer and then Marguerite broke off to make coffee. Luc drank quickly, shook our hands, clapped me on the shoulder and slid out of the flat door with a wave. Marguerite came towards me, held me by both arms and said:

'Welcome again.'

I remember blushing.

Later, after a simple meal of meat and potatoes she excused herself and explained that she had to go out to see someone. I said I would wash up, in French, which brought a laugh from her, a rarity indeed!

'You learn well!' she replied.

I had much to ask her about the conversation with Luc but this was not the time. Having seen her out of the door, again with the finger to her lips, I cleaned up in the kitchen and once more sat waiting for the next move; realising that this was going to be the name of the game for some considerable while.

Marguerite returned and stood by the flat door, waving me away as I looked out of the salon. Minutes later a man appeared who I remembered as Jules, one of the men who had questioned me in the church. We each took a seat in the salon and Jules wasted no time. 'The other group send you back because they have no plan. We know a lady who is leading some young Frenchmen to Holland to join de Gaulle and we hope she will take you. Meantime you must stay here. If you want things ask Marguerite.'

I thanked Jules for what he was doing and asked if his group would tell the British that I was alive in Paris. He gave a non-committal grunt followed by 'Perhaps', nodded to Marguerite and made his own way out of the flat.

We sat in silence for a moment and then I said, 'I'm afraid the other group kept your coat and trousers.'

Marguerite smiled 'No matter. You look better now.'

I felt emboldened to ask, 'Is Luc part of your group? I did not know he had a gun.'

She waited a few seconds before replying, 'No. He works for the others. He tells me he stole the gun from a German on the Metro going to collect you.'

Some fellow, I thought, but then all these people were who were putting their lives at risk in keeping the Resistance going. Not that I was going to hear any more about them that night because Marguerite was up and in the kitchen busily sorting out the camp bed again. We had more coffee and she produced the self-same pyjamas wishing me '*Dormez bien.*' Almost like being back home, except that I began to wonder how my folks back in England were bearing up.

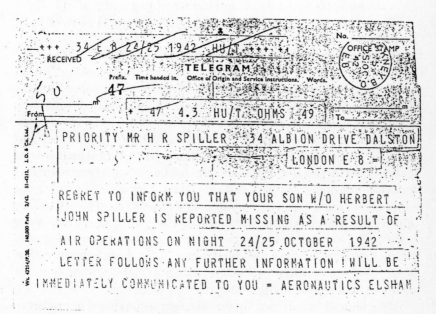

The next few days slipped into a routine with Marguerite out early leaving me something for breakfast, and also a cold lunch to save her a journey. In return I cleaned the flat as silently as I could and read everything I could find including the labels on the packets of food in the kitchen, which wasn't a long task, as she hadn't much. The days were a little cool though and I wore everything I had. The evenings were better, with a good fire going and some happy hours teaching each other our mother tongues. It was cosy and very innocent and I came to look forward to her return. In other circumstances it could, I suppose, have led to an indiscretion, but the overshadowing presence of propriety and the possible repercussions if the occurrence of anything dishonourable had come to the attention of the group, happily prevented me from losing my head. Although it very nearly happened one night when I was shaken from sleep by the sound of gunfire in the distance, and the reverberation of bombs.

I slipped into the salon and drew the curtains to see several searchlight cones, heavy flak and the distant ground flashes of bombs. The din was deafening and as I watched dumbfounded I felt a touch on my shoulder. It was Marguerite in her dressing gown looking like a startled rabbit and shaking visibly. I naturally pulled her towards me and we clung together during the whole of the raid, until the noise had died down and her trembling had ceased.

I kissed her forehead and said, 'Are you all right? The RAF have no manners.'

She gave me a wan smile. 'Yes. I hope they did well.'

It was an affectionate moment when things could have got out of hand but it passed and Marguerite said, 'How about coffee?' It was so incongruous, we burst out laughing as we let go of each other.

Perhaps it was just as well that two days afterwards, word came from Jules that the lady guide was getting ready for her journey and that she had consented to my inclusion in the party which was to leave within forty-eight hours. During the day when Marguerite was at work the hours seemed endless and I began to fall victim to impatience. Even our evening language exchange lacked enthusiasm and we just stared into the fire knowing that our brief acquaintance was coming to an end. I remarked on the fact that coal seemed easy to come by and felt very ashamed when Marguerite explained that other members of the group had given up part of their ration so that I could be kept in reasonable comfort.

Abbé Dufour brightened up our evening by paying a brief visit to say goodbye and to tell me to be ready at six o'clock next morning. He also handed me a *carte d'identité* with a dubious photo in it indicating that I was René Martoux, a farm worker from Aubigny. Marguerite was to take me to the Gare de l'Est railway station before she went to work and hand me over to the lady guide who would be alone, the young Frenchmen being dispersed around the station to appear just before the train was due to leave. With luck we should be in England in three days.

Since there was no alcohol in the flat we celebrated with the inevitable coffee. Try as I might I had no sleep that night and it seemed that only an hour had passed before Marguerite appeared to waken me. She was surprised that I had not slept, but immediately busied herself preparing a light breakfast whilst I washed and shaved and put on my things. We ate in complete silence just looking at each other and occasionally smiling.

'Come,' she suddenly said, 'we must go now.'

I just had time to shoulder my haversack and give one more glance around the flat, as if to memorise it, and we were outside in a damp grey half darkness. Entering the Metro I felt a little apprehensive about meeting any occupying troops but soon realised that it was far too early for that. The trip to the station was quite uneventful, with Marguerite openly holding my hand to throw off any suspecting onlookers.

The entrance to the station seemed to be filled with people scurrying hither and thither, most surprising to me for that time in the morning, but it was a useful cover. Marguerite motioned for me to stop by a small kiosk selling papers and hurried off into the main hall. I ambled about a little bit as if waiting for someone to arrive, and must admit that I had the same feeling as when the priest left me at St Dizier. It was short-lived. Marguerite came back through the crowd with a small lady dressed fiercely in black, with piercing green eyes and the hint of a moustache on her top lip. She looked me up and down as Marguerite introduced us.

'Herbert, this is Madame Verdain. *Madame Verdain, Herbert.*'

I grabbed her hand and on the spur of the moment bent down and kissed it. She pulled her hand away roughly but there was a smile in her eyes. *'Bien,'* she said. *'Au revoir, Marguerite.'*

Duly dismissed, Marguerite looked a little disconsolate, there was a brief moment as she struggled to keep her composure and then she held my face and kissed me fully on the lips. *'Adieu,'* she whispered and walked off.

# CHAPTER SIX

# To Holland

Before I could recover from my embarrassment and sadness at Marguerite's impulsive farewell, I found Madame Verdain tugging at my arm. Giving her a quick glance I noticed that her eyes had assumed an all-knowing look and that she had misunderstood the kiss completely. Or perhaps I had; it gave me pause for thought on several occasions on our journey.

There was little time to dwell on the matter right at the moment as I was being pushed along through pockets of people carrying all manner of baggage and, without exception, gesticulating wildly. Trains were hissing and puffing impatiently and it seemed that the whole world was on the move. The passengers had that same wild desire to get away from their present surroundings as we had seen in the refugees filling the roads in 1940 as they fled from the advancing Germans. Maybe the RAF raids on Paris were panicking the populace into leaving for quieter country places. Whatever was going on it was certainly extremely useful to someone like Madame Verdain organising a mass escape plan; the general turmoil was an excellent cover for a group to move about in.

We stopped in front of a platform gateway crowded with people waving tickets. A crackling loudspeaker gave out a message of some sort in a rumbling monotone. Gradually one by one young men began attaching themselves to the formidable presence of Madame Verdain and she spent some time giving them instructions in her strident voice which needed no amplification even in the rising noise about us. Two young men were singled out by her and introduced to me. André was another tall, blond Frenchman with an angular face and jutting chin. His fresh face and laughing blue eyes placed him as a typical student. Marc was more of the Latin, dark thick hair and olive-skinned, a pseudo-moustache seemed to be out of context on his open honest face. Madame Verdain spelt out their duties in a few words. They were to stay with me at all times and to prevent people talking to me. Fortunately they had both had experience in speaking English, in the various youth hostels in the south of England which they had visited as students, which together with my fractured

French served as a reasonable method of communication.

Having got her group sorted out Madame Verdain motioned to us to move towards the platform entrance. She had some form of blanket ticket to cover all of us, which seemed perfectly acceptable to the man on the barrier, although he was giving the group a hard look as we went through. I never discovered exactly what sort of permit we were travelling under, but the mere sight of that tough and capable woman would have caused any person in minor authority to accept her explanations without demur. Certainly I never saw at any stage on the journey any one of the lads in our group ever dispute her commands or directions. No doubt she must have told them that they either did what she wanted or they could find their own way out of France.

Everyone moved towards the empty carriages at the front of the train which were of the open type containing sixty or seventy seats, and these were soon taken up, with people also standing. I managed a corner seat with André and Marc on my left and the rest of the group were in various other positions but not all together. Madame Verdain sat amongst a number of the ordinary travellers, markedly in isolation. The idea was that if there were any unexpected control points on the journey and any one of the group were interrogated or found to have any discrepancy in their papers that they were not to reveal any others of their group and especially Madame Verdain or myself. I decided that I would feign sleep, as I had done on the way to Paris, for at least the first part of the journey until all the passengers had settled down, and I curled into the corner wondering when or how we would get something to eat.

Most people were crowding on, treading on the feet of the sitters and it became impossible not to show some irritation, although I limited myself to annoyed glances. Fortunately a railway official threw open the carriage door and with little ceremony pulled half a dozen travellers off the train amid cries of despair. Looking across at the man seated opposite with what looked like his young family I smiled in sympathy and nearly provoked a crisis. He leaned forward and said something in rapid French which I didn't catch and I froze horrified. André, ever alert, leant across me and went into a brief explanation in which I caught the words *sourd et muet*, or deaf and dumb. For the next forty-eight hours I was to hear those words on a number of occasions and it grew to be a huge joke with André and Marc. The man seemed immediately satisfied and leant over and patted my shoulder amicably.

The train got off to a slow grinding start and I watched with some sadness as the surroundings of Paris slowly slipped away. The feeling, that I was leaving all those good people who had helped me and who would face a further period of oppression, was very strong in my mind, and I wished them well until such time as they were liberated. Time passed and the fields began and I assumed my sleeping position against the carriage window. It was impossible to keep that up for long since we were stopping at virtually every small station or level crossing. The consequent jolting of the carriages put paid to anyone trying to sleep, or pretending to as in my case. The man opposite produced the answer for me quite unwittingly. He tapped my knee, smiled and produced a crumpled newspaper. Thoughts raced through my mind; well I was deaf and dumb but obviously not blind and I suppose I could have been taught to read. It was worth a shot anyway and André who was looking on was unperturbed. Smiling at the man, I nodded and took the paper from him.

It lasted me a long time, a very long time in fact as the train was slowed at times almost to a halt. Much to my amazement it went backwards two or three times to the shouted comments of my fellow passengers leaning out of the windows and berating the driver. Eventually some sidings appeared and we pulled up at a larger and more busy station. André nudged me with his knee, Madame Verdain was up and departing. I felt sticky and hungry yet relieved that things were happening. Politely I bowed to the man opposite, gave him back his newspaper and followed André and Marc out onto the platform.

Madame Verdain swept off with her convoy behind her in twos and threes at respectable distances. Across other platforms and finally over a bridge to another smaller platform on the far side of the sidings. Two railwaymen met her there and led her to an empty waiting room or more properly, a waiting shed. Here we all congregated and bread, cheese and wine appeared, presumably brought by the railwaymen who must have been part of Madame Verdain's group, or allied to it. The chatter was considerable but the voice of Madame Verdain cut through it easily. We were to remain there for two hours until another connection arrived. There was little comfort afforded by the narrow bench seating in the shed so we used our bags and coats and sprawled where there was room on the floor. Madame Verdain singled out our three and gave André some quick and precise instructions. She had seen the sticky moment with the friendly passenger and was worried in case a similar thing occurred. In future we would sit in at least sixes, three each side, with me in the centre, thus cutting out any direct contact with other passengers. Also the deaf and dumb play had to go, I would be more natural as a person who said little. André and Marc nodded to her and she went off to give lectures and commands to others who needed it. We settled back down again and whiled away the minutes.

It was nearer three hours before we were once more collected by Madame Verdain and hustled across the bridge on the reverse journey to the original platform. It was early afternoon and not a great deal of passengers were about, all those we saw were country people in various permutations of rustic garb. No one seemed to think that our group of young men were of any interest. The train arrived and we were delighted to find that the carriages were divided into individual compartments with room for six each side. A dozen of us pushed in amid taunts and laughter, mostly about the fact that our female mentor was next door and we could relax for the first time since leaving Paris.

It was during the next few hours that I was introduced to a number of French students songs, all risqué but the tunes and words were easily memorised. It all helped to make me feel more secure in that I was becoming able to pronounce and use the language. Not that one could burst into this kind of song on any occasion; something more genteel was called for and I asked André to teach me some easy popular songs. There was a great deal of back-chat and gaiety and choosing and eventually I was tutored in '*Les Amis de la Table Ronde*', '*Trois Compagnons*' and '*Tout va très bien, Madame la Marquise*'. If nothing else I could move along country roads singing the odd song and allaying suspicion thereby.

The train jerked to the umpteenth stop and we were waved to silence by the lad sitting at the rear window. '*Boches*,' he whispered and pointed forward along the track. Guttural cries were coming from that direction and a river of excited French voices. My companions looked at each other anxiously and André spoke softly in an ordered tone of authority which rather surprised me. Everybody sat back in their seats looking straight ahead. 'Stay calm. Say nothing,' murmured André to me.

What a stroke of good luck it was that the Germans were checking papers starting from the front of the train. This meant that they were reaching Madame Verdain before us, and it wasn't long before we could hear that dear lady's voice, not raised in anger but almost like

an officer of high rank. What explanation she was giving and what
papers she was carrying I never found out, but when the door opened
and a young soldier with a coal-scuttle helmet climbed in he asked
but one lad for his '*Papieren*', checked the identity card, gave the rest
of us a sneer and stamped out again.

'*Formidable*', cried André and smacked his knee.

The rest including myself collapsed in nervous laughter. We had a
long anxious wait whilst the rest of the train was checked but
eventually we moved off into more rolling country. At the next stop,
Madame Verdain appeared in the doorway to say that we were in
Belgium and disembarking in half an hour. She was as imperturb-
able as ever and obviously enjoying her odyssey. As if to throw off the
nervous tension caused by the search, the carriage occupants broke
into a series of individual chats and I managed to get André to talk
about them. He told me that they were all workers in an electric light
bulb factory who had decided to join de Gaulle. Before they left the
factory they had sabotaged as many of the bulbs as they could, at
least two months' production, all of which would have otherwise
found its way into Germany. He was very proud of the fact but said
that he was worried about his family and whether his involvement in
the sabotage would put them in any danger. I looked at his long lean
face and felt that de Gaulle would be more than pleased to have him
and his like in the Free French Forces.

Another stop and Madame Verdain appeared again to order us off
the train, once again in two's and three's. The station seemed like the
back of nowhere and we followed Madame Verdain out of a wide
gate with a station official looking at us in amusement. After a short
walk we were congregating again on the side of the main road and
after a ten minute wait we all boarded a dilapidated bus which eased
its way over the uneven road in no apparent hurry to get anywhere.
One or two small hamlets went by before Madame Verdain went
forward and spoke to the driver. The bus stopped by a high hedge
and we disembarked with some good humour. A cart track led off to
the left and we all had our work cut out keeping up with Madame
Verdain as she strode purposefully to her destination. A short
thickset farmer with a red jolly face welcomed us at his farm gate and
waved us in walking ahead of us to a large hay barn. The door was
already open, the hay inviting and we threw down our few chattels
and flung ourselves into the sweet smelling mass. It was to be our
dormitory for the night and we spent some time digging out a nest for
ourselves. Supper came in a big metal cooking pot, with several

loaves and coffee in tin mugs. A memorable meal made even more remarkable by the information given to us by Madame Verdain that we should be inside Holland early next day.

The same young girls who had brought the food came to clear away and to tell us that we were welcome in the farmhouse now that it was dark. We drifted over in small groups to be directed by Madame Verdain to a large inner room containing various oddments of furniture stacked in piles. The room was obviously used only as a store but was ideal for the purpose of accommodating our number. In short time we were at home in old chairs, sofas or chaises longues, or on dusty cushions. The farmer came in with his family, introduced them without mentioning names and then distributed packets of dark Belgian tobacco and loosely filled cigarettes. I was never at home with the coarse tasting cigarettes, but I persevered, in the knowledge that with the occasional 'fag-end' stuck in my mouth I would look less like an alien.

Many questions were being asked in the general hubbub but neither the farmer nor his family were anxious to talk about themselves, I suspected that they had been briefed by Madame Verdain earlier. The two girls who we learnt were the daughters went off and later returned with glasses and wine and we were each given one glassful. The wine then disappeared, again I supposed on the instructions of Madame Verdain who was taking no chances. A round of toasts saw our ration of wine off. Shortly afterwards we were whisked off to the barn to get plenty of sleep for the next day's adventure.

I knew nothing more until I was being roughly shaken by André. 'Wake up', he said laughing. 'Wash outside.'

Several of the lads were already out there scooping water out of a large drum between the farm buildings. Avoiding most of the horseplay I managed to splash enough water on my face and bare chest and dry myself on the coarse brown towel Marguerite had put in my haversack. By the time I returned to the barn Madame Verdain had arrived with the two girls bearing more loaves and coffee. She cried for silence and then spat out two or three quick sentences in rapid French. Grabbing the two girls she stamped off into the farmhouse. André looked at me and knew I hadn't absorbed what she had said. 'We go in half an hour,' he explained. I don't know why but for the first time since leaving Paris, I felt nervous anticipation of the next step.

It was totally unfounded. We were assembled again in front of the barn whilst Madame Verdain gave her daily orders and then, in the same two's and three's, followed her back up the cart track to the road beyond at regular intervals. This time the farmer and his family were not present to wave us off; it seemed that everything had been thought of and that any watchers would have little cause for suspicion. We looked a motley throng stretched out along the roadside, and it was some minutes after the last couple had emerged to take up their station before the same dilapidated bus coughed to a halt opposite Madame Verdain. She stood by the driver as we pushed past her to the seats beyond. There was only one other passenger already on the bus, an elderly lady eating an apple. It was far too early for the local residents, I thought, but then it occurred to me that this might not be a scheduled bus at all, and that the old lady was a blind. My confidence was returning and I warmed once again to Madame Verdain's organisation.

By the time that we had arrived I had already worked out that the smiling official would be on duty at the railway station and so it came to pass. Another mark to Madame Verdain. We all passed through the gateway onto the platform and stood around in various places ready to assemble quickly when the train came. Other passengers were arriving and we had to change position once or twice to ensure we would enter the train in the right groups. I was hoping that, as before, we would get individual compartments but as the train steamed in it was obvious that the open type of carriage was being used. When it stopped there was a general free for all as everyone fought to get to the seats first and we lost a lot of friends in those brief minutes by the physical way in which we made certain of our seats.

As the clamour died down, I could see that André myself and Marc were sitting opposite the three lads detailed by Madame Verdain to make up our six. I marvelled at the strength of her personality that forced these lads to do her bidding rather than face her wrath. The hostility of our unsuccessful fellow passengers was easy to live with in comparison and I felt secure between my fellow escapers.

Little Belgium rolled by as the train made its way grudgingly through a series of small villages and towns. Farming seemed to be continuing as normal in its own quiet fashion and the roads were much busier in terms of traffic, probably being that much nearer Germany. More and more troops could be seen on the railway stations but none were attempting to get on our train which presumably was a local one serving rural communities. There was no recurrence of the joyful song session that we had had on the previous train, the lads preferring to pass the time in dozing and quiet conversation. Before long the rolling fields gave way to growing numbers of houses. We were about to run into a large town and again I marvelled at Madame Verdain's cheek in going right in to the lion's mouth. As before I hadn't reckoned on the quality of her pre-planning. As the train drew to a halt I saw a name-plate bearing the word 'Gand' above the station platform. It meant nothing to me then but later I knew that I had passed through Ghent, to where the good news was taken by the rider from Aix in the famous poem.

We sat tight until Madame Verdain rose demurely and made her unhurried way onto the platform. She stayed outside looking up and down the platform and then nodded to us to get out. As I looked towards the far end of the platform I could see quite a press of German servicemen forming into disciplined groups under the commands of their superiors, but Madame Verdain did not seem concerned with that. She passed a quick word for us to string out along the opposite side of the platform in our now customary two's and three's. Ten minutes or so later we were boarding another down at heel train packed with civilians, thankfully with seats still to fill. The train waited for an agonising half hour before moving off, but in the end we were through Ghent into open country again, without having to pass a barrier.

The lads must have felt relieved by the ease with which we were passing through the various obstacles in our path because once again their voices began to be raised in song. Most of the other passengers were looking amused so I assumed that apart from the songs which I now knew, the others were also of an acceptable nature. I joined in where I could until the jollity was called to a halt by the departure of Madame Verdain this time as the train stopped at a tiny country stopping place. We followed her off the train and out onto the road beyond without seeing another soul. In our usual pattern of small groups we walked for well over an hour working up quite a thirst which we were hoping would soon be slaked. Madame Verdain's route was full of twists and turns, first small roads then cart tracks then back to small roads again, finally passing through a small village which we all thought would be our 'oasis'.

We were disappointed as she led us through the village and out again for some way before pulling us off the road into a small copse. André passed on to me the gist of Madame Verdain's instructions as we lay in the undergrowth. 'We are waiting for the villagers who cross the border regularly, at about an hour from now. They are rarely, if ever, stopped or searched because they return after an hour having made simple purchases or exchanged something. We will join with them and meet up in the village beyond.' I shook my head in amazement, and mentally promised myself that until I got back home I would use a similar bold approach whenever faced with a sticky moment.

People began passing by the copse well before an hour had passed and we were waved to go ahead by Madame Verdain. There was no time for nervousness, we filtered into the throng from a side track next to the copse and sauntered along at the same pace as the villagers who gave no sign that we were out of the ordinary accepting us as being from some other village, no doubt. My heart went into my mouth as we turned the bend beyond the copse and the border post across the road came clearly into view. The slow pace was doing nothing for my nerves. I hung my head in an unconscious effort to hide myself and shambled on. The hinged post went up as the first people arrived at it and hardly daring to look I knew that we were home and dry as we all pressed forward.

A few yards ahead a similar post signified the gateway to Holland and miraculously this went up as if to welcome all refugees to the bosom of the Netherlands. No one raised a voice above the gentle murmur of conversation of the passing walkers and much like Alice we passed under the post into a new country, full of wonderment and relief. Another few hundred yards and we were in a fairly large village gathering around Madame Verdain, to be then split up into smaller groups and distributed around the three cafés in the main street. Welcome food and drink appeared and we put it all away in very quick time, wondering what would happen next.

We were not kept in suspense. Madame Verdain came into the cafe and paid the bill, beckoning to André. They stood speaking in agitated tones for a short while and then she left swiftly looking strangely perturbed.

André came over to our table and whispered to me, 'We are going back.'

He then spoke quickly to the others and we went outside to find the rest of the lads who were by then emerging from the other cafés. I pieced together what had happened. Apparently parachutists had landed the previous night near the town where we were intending to embark from and the Germans were in a state of alarm and were commencing to search all buildings in a radius which included the village we were in. The situation was far too critical for Madame Verdain so she was removing us from the sensitive area into another area where we might try a fresh run.

Thus, after the high moments of the past hour, we found ourselves retracing our steps among the self same villagers as before and in a short time we were back in Belgium passing the copse and making our way back to the country railway platform we had hopefully started from. It was well before noon, there were no other passengers, and the recent events had tired us not a little. We slipped to the ground and cat-napped easily, only to be woken by Madame Verdain who was anxious to get us over the line to the platform on the opposite side. As she expected, a much larger train emerged out of the distance picked us up and sped on at a fair pace. We stood in the corridor occasionally glancing at the seated passengers, a sprinkling of whom were Germans. Perhaps the main trains would allow us to travel faster, I thought, at least it was a change.

We changed trains three times after that, twice in large towns after Madame Verdain had arranged our tickets using whatever permit she had. It held up to inspection nevertheless because we passed several gates and barriers in the process. As for ourselves we just laid back and dozed, the occasional traveller looked into our carriage and decided against it, quite properly I would say, as we must by then have looked unkempt ruffians.

The day wore on, each stop we made brought a hope that this might be the end of the journey, our tails were a little bit down having nearly made it the first time. Almost, as if in apology, Madame Verdain finally entered our carriage to say that we would be getting out at the next stop. Bleary-eyed and yawning we wiped the condensation from the carriage windows as we pulled in at last. A white post on the platform had a sign underneath 'Momignies', and it was raining.

Once again we made our way out of a station, openly and without any trouble. Madame Verdain led us towards a gate in a high wall which opened onto a courtyard. Two men emerged from a building waved us over and shook hands all round. We were told that we had a two-hour walk ahead of us but that we would be safely hidden on arrival. After the day's events we were grateful for any shelter and being young and fairly durable we all declared that we were able to make the journey.

We had to make our way through dense forest after we had left the village and those who had flimsy footwear soon found that the mud and thick leaves were playing havoc with them. I felt fairly comfortable and the drizzle falling through the trees was not penetrating my coat. You could just make out the people in front of you at times and it was quite easy to walk into the occasional tree. Eventually we crossed a railway line, the same, as it happened, as the one we came in on, and immediately were swallowed up again in the darkness of the trees. It became just an exercise in putting one foot in front of the other, interminably, in cold wet and muddy anonymity. The effect was eerie, there was no sound of any kind except the sucking sound of feet being pulled out of wet leaves and mud, and you began to wonder about walking in circles. Such thoughts, of course, were an insult to the very capable, tough and resourceful characters who were leading us. In retrospect, I cannot remember wondering how Madame Verdain was faring; such is the selfishness of personal survival.

Breaking through the last of the trees we took to the road before us and downhill saw a sprinkle of houses indicating civilisation of some sort. As we made our way downhill further houses began to appear, then a crossroads, then a café, closed though at that hour. Word came to keep noise to a minimum, the curfew was being strictly maintained. The two men leading tapped at the café door which opened after a few moments. As silently as we could we slipped through the door and I remember the wonderful smells of coffee and wine and all the typical café odours. We slumped into various hard wooden chairs and lay across the small round tables. The two men looked over and laughed.

'*Bienvenu,*' one said. '*Vous êtes en France.*'

The café owner's wife bustled around with cups of coffee and cognac and Madame Verdain told us we had crossed the border into France and were in the outskirts of Fourmies, a small industrial town. Later we would be split up and billeted with members of the Resistance, and at no time were we to endanger them by attempting any individual escape. Patience was now important until such time as arrangements could be made to continue our progress to England.

# CHAPTER SEVEN

# Fourmies

After a simple meal of cheese and bread we took turns to clean ourselves up in the back kitchen and damp clothes were everywhere. Several blankets and heavy coats were brought in to the main café room and everyone of our party made a makeshift bed on the floor with whatever came to hand. Madame Verdain was taken upstairs into more comfortable quarters and no one begrudged her that. The night passed quickly and we were woken early to clear the main café room for business. We crowded into a sitting room at the back of the café for hot bread and coffee. Madame Verdain came down to share our breakfast in a hurried fashion, embraced us all and said she was returning to Paris. Our safety would be in the hands of the local Resistance who were in contact with people who could help us. In her usual style she betrayed no emotion, which is more than I can say for the young men who surrounded her for the last time. As she was leaving I grabbed her hand and kissed it as I had done in Paris.

'*Bien*,' she growled. '*Au revoir tous.*'

After that, strange men began to arrive at intervals to take away one or two of the party. It was rather like 'Ten green bottles' and it wasn't long before I was shaking the hands of André and Marc and expressing the hope that I would soon see them again. Eventually I was left with the café owner's wife who offered me more coffee and some thick brown sandwiches.

Before I had finished them the café owner came in with two middle-aged short thick-set men wearing thick blue coats over muddy overalls. They came towards me, shook hands and introduced themselves as Antoine and Edouard and immediately held up my short coat for me to put on. Their whole demeanour was brisk and purposeful, a nod of the head was enough for me to follow them without demur. In the main room of the café we passed through a maze of tables each surrounded by a seated jabbering clique of workmen totally uninterested in our progress, and out into pale November sunlight.

The streets were quite busy with people cycling and walking to their various work-places and my companions occasionally waved to a friend as we passed along. I was surprised to see that apart from the occasional military lorry, there was no sign of German soldiery in the town. It was fairly early, of course, and no doubt the best time to move people like myself through the streets. We stopped outside another café and the two men engaged in some quiet conversation. Eventually Edouard shook my hand and went inside. Immediately Antoine tugged at my elbow and nodded towards another road across the other side forking away to the right.

As we turned the corner I caught sight of the road name 'Rue de l'Espérance' or 'Hope Road' and silently gave birth to the thought that this might be a good omen. It was uphill most of the way and as we progressed the houses on our left fell away leaving a row of cottages on the right side of the road opposite open cultivated land. It was here that Antoine finally touched my elbow and steered me to one of the cottage doors. We entered a passage with rooms off to the right leading through to a back dining room.

Here waiting for us was Antoine's wife Judith, a kindly gentle soul, who held my hand and kissed my cheek in warm welcome and whispered, '*Pauvre petit*' in a gesture of sympathy. I learnt later that she had done sterling work for the Resistance in the First World War and had been decorated for her efforts, and that beneath the benign shell of the typical French mother she had an iron determination and a passionate desire to serve France in whatever way she could.

Looking at her, demurely dressed in black, her head neatly crowned with soft straight brown hair wound up in a bun it seemed impossible to read into her pleasant placid face a tenacity which her exploits had obviously required. Antoine standing alongside her, sporting a good day's white bristle on his heart-shaped Gallic face, and a grey military moustache, looked much more the part of the tough rustic. Despite their obvious differences, their loving regard for each other was immediately apparent and they seemed quite ready to share the dangers of their actions together. Unfortunately for me, neither spoke English, for I would have loved to have got to know them more, but the few French words I could now muster were enough to see us through normal day to day matters.

Judith busied herself making coffee whilst Antoine took me into an inner room. This was to be my room during my stay there and I was not to leave it unless called to do so by the family. There was a lovely old soft high bed, marble-topped wash stand and bowl, armchair and other knick knacks. Large brown photographs hung framed around the walls, and a woolly rug covered most of the floor. It was never mentioned, but I am sure that this was their own room and that they were giving it up for me; it would be so like them. More importantly I suppose from their point of view, was the fact that there was no window through which any nosy neighbour could peer. It was cosy and comfortable and I got to love its feeling of safety and protection.

Over coffee I discovered that there were two children, their son, Fabien, a seventeen-year-old factory worker, and daughter Judith, a schoolgirl of thirteen. Both would be coming home later but Judith produced family photographs to enable me to identify them when they came. Antoine then remarked that my clothes needed washing and I was taken back to the inner room to change into various oddments of clothing and underwear, by the look of it, Fabien's. At least it was gloriously soft and I lay on the bed reading an old magazine until called into the back room for lunch. A heaped bowl of soup and vegetables did wonders for my appetite and I was half way through a kind of cake when there was knocking at the front door.

There was no panic, in fact Judith continued to eat without even looking up. Antoine smiled and motioned for me to go into the inner room, then moved up the passage towards the front door. I could hear raised voices and laughter and people moving up and down. There was nothing to do but to sit in the armchair for at least an hour whilst the sound of voices continued. Eventually the obvious noises of departure filtered into the room and shortly afterwards the gratifying clunk of the closing front door.

Antoine came in to explain that it was one of his cousins visiting Fourmies who had dropped in on the off-chance. The surprise visit had, however, made him have second thoughts and he said that as the front door was always unlocked and neighbours were likely to call in from time to time it would be better for me to keep to my room during the day and come out in the evening to share the family meal. My heart sank at the thought of being stuck in one room for the best part of the day, but it quickly occurred to me that these good people were running a terrible risk in sheltering me, and it wasn't as if the room was uncomfortable. I confirmed that I understood and Antoine gripped my shoulder heavily in an impulsive show of pleasure and affection. Judith brought in the rest of my meal and for a moment they both sat on the bed and discussed my welfare.

Alone again, I began to pass the time deciphering an old French book and rolling a number of cigarettes. Time was going to hang pretty heavily, but I was determined not to get bored or impatient. I had no idea what Antoine's occupation was, but it wouldn't be practicable for him to be around keeping me company every day, and it was important that I should keep myself interested for long periods.

Part of this problem was soon solved as I was introduced to a small black dog named Poupette, the family pet with whom I struck up an immediate relationship. She stayed with me for hours on end and I was grateful for her company. At times she would scratch at the door to be let out and I had to be careful to make sure that there were no visitors in the outer rooms, before opening the door, otherwise it might have looked suspicious indeed if a dog had appeared to have let itself out.

Later that afternoon I could hear the front door being used and once again settled down for a silent period. But in a matter of moments Antoine appeared with a solemn young girl, a miniature of her mother, and introduced her to me as Judith. She was clearly suspicious, shy and possibly frightened, and I was a little disconcerted at her steady stare of distrust. It would take some time to break that down by the look of it. Antoine warned her not to speak of me to anyone, and after sparing me a grudging '*Monsieur*' she backed out of the room. As Antoine turned to leave he said that Fabien would be home in a couple of hours when we would all eat.

Fabien was a different kettle of fish. He came into the room unannounced, a tall young lad with black brushed back hair atop a strong pallid face. He was very excited and eager to meet me. 'I am Fabien,' he roared in English, but that was all he could manage. We lapsed into my method of speaking French in short sentences and in no time we had agreed to teach each other our native tongues. He laughed at my efforts at rolling cigarettes and we spent the time before the evening meal re-rolling them French fashion.

Sitting around the table in the backroom I really felt part of this family although I had only been there for a day. The table was plentifully filled with bowls of vegetables and bread and we were each given a large portion of rabbit. I reflected that the city dwellers were perhaps not as well off for food as their country counterparts and this was borne out when Antoine explained to me that they owned a small holding and had chickens and rabbits, and all we were eating was their own. The younger Judith spent her time slyly watching me out of the corner of her eye, but she would not respond to any of my attempts to break down the awkwardness between us.

Later when the table was clear she sat in interested silence as

Fabien produced his English grammar book and we began to concoct from it some simple exercises in pronunciation and grammar.
Antoine and Judith were in a high state of merriment at Fabien's
efforts and occasionally butted in to put me right on some of my
French accents. It all seemed far distant from the real danger which
was lurking outside. Our light-hearted moment lasted until Antoine
reminded Fabien that he had to rise early for work. Reluctantly we
made our way to bed, having cemented some good Anglo-French
relations. Slipping into that soft high bed I realised that I hadn't had
such comfort since living at the wine shop in Paris. Sleep soon caught
up with me.

The days after that dragged interminably except for the weekends
when Antoine and Fabien were at home all day. I busied myself with
the French grammar book which took longer than I imagined since
the instructions were all in French and I had to reverse the teaching
to make sense of it all. Nevertheless Fabien and I made great strides
in our learning, he progressed to some simple English songs
including 'Nellie Dean' and 'Moonlight Bay', and I began talking
French in longer sentences, although he insisted that my accent was
more Polish than French. We grew very close, almost like brothers,
which did not improve relations with the younger Judith.

One day Antoine brought me a parcel from an anonymous donor
which contained some Belgian chocolate, cigarettes and some uncut
black Belgian tobacco. I passed the tobacco on to Antoine for his
pipe, shared the chocolate with the two Judiths, and Fabien and I
scoffed the rest smoking ourselves to death in the bargain! What
slight show of affection I received from the younger Judith for sharing
my chocolate was dashed in a very short time when I broke off a piece
and gave it to the dog Poupette. With chocolate in such short supply
I had unwittingly committed a cardinal sin in her eyes and she
jumped up in a rage from the table and stamped out of the room. Her
mother shaking her head and smiling followed the younger Judith
out of the room, coming back later to pat my shoulder and to say that
the moment had passed over.

In actual fact Judith told me that the young girl was amused at my
relationship with the dog whom I used to greet every morning with
'*Bonjour, Mademoiselle Poupette*'. After the chocolate incident she
began to soften in her attitude towards me. Antoine probably had
something to do with it as well, because he was ever concerned about
the possibility that a chance remark might betray my whereabouts,
and an angry schoolgirl might just say something to a friend.

Whatever it was the atmosphere began to lighten and I got completely accepted.

Every now and then in the evening before the curfew, Antoine, and also Fabien at times, used to escort me out of doors for a walk along the less frequented roads, strolling in the normal way while they chatted about this and that. My role was more or less as a silent partner but I was able to throw in a question every now and then. I learnt that Antoine had served throughout the First World War as a soldier and had come through many months of harrowing experience in the hell-hole of Verdun. He was now 51, looking perhaps a lot older because of that experience, but his grizzled sunburnt face and keen far-seeing eyes, inspired confidence in me and I was glad to have his kind of strength on my side. Both he and Edouard were members of a Resistance group, but my future was not in their hands. They were in contact with a larger group based in Belgium who were in the business of returning Allied airmen to England and I had to wait until many matters had been settled before they would be able to pass me on.

One evening we were joined by Edouard and taken to a quiet little café on the edge of the town. It was a cold night and I was introduced to a large glass of marc, a potent drink made out of the skins of champagne grapes, well loved by the soldiers of the French Army. Antoine and Edouard quietly discussed their plans before opening out into more general conversation.

Some workers came in and one detached himself from the group to pass the time of day with Antoine and Edouard. He looked across at me and phrases in the local patois crackled out of his mouth. It was gobbledegook to me, but before I could respond Antoine trotted out the familiar phrase '*sourd et muet*' and with a shrug the man moved away. I drank the rest of the marc in one gulp spluttering helplessly as the fiery liquid seared my throat. My companions gave a hearty laugh, shouted a goodbye to the café owner and steered me outside. We hurried away with Antoine explaining that they had been waiting for another contact; unhappily the man who had stopped at the table was a suspected collaborator, so they deemed it best to leave.

That was the end of our nocturnal excursions; the risk of contact with suspicious or even curious people was far too great for Antoine and his family to run and it was decided that any outside contacts would have to come to Antoine's house to see me. Apparently the Belgian organisation were interested in my whereabouts but before taking any step to move me, they wanted one of their members to interrogate me and check my authenticity. Several of their members had been arrested and imprisoned within the last few weeks, having been betrayed by agents impersonating Allied airmen and matters were extremely critical. No moves were being made to continue the collection of Allied airmen being hidden in various parts of France and Belgium, until the organisation were perfectly certain that the airmen were bona fide.

So back to my room I went to further my study of the French tongue and to wait for the promised visit of the organisation's emissary. After a few days a man did call at the house to tell us that my story had been checked back as far as St Dizier and that it would not be necessary for me to be seen before moving to Belgium. Contact had been made with London and a code phrase had been given to the move and this would be announced on the Free Radio when all was ready. The organisation had arranged the use of the code phrases to inspire confidence in the members that the resources of the Allies was behind them. The phrases were included in a series of '*Messages personnels*' and were quite meaningless to German ears. The phrase we had to listen for was '*Très bon pour chocolat*', and this meant that a radio watch had to be maintained every evening after that.

This news was, of course, very exciting for me as I could sense that I was once again under service orders and all I had to do was sit tight and the rescue would be put into operation by the RAF. Before he left the man said he was hoping to make contact with some Swiss helpers and that if I had a message for my family he would see to it that it was passed on through the Swiss Consul. I racked my brains to concoct a simple message which did not compromise anyone and handed the note to the man who read it carefully and then nodded all round.

'*Salut,*' he said and slipped out into the night.

Antoine and Judith were also very excited and they had some very heated conversations as to who would be responsible for listening to the radio late into the evening. Although it was forbidden by the Germans to listen to Allied broadcasts there were few French people who did not take the risk to hear the famous V for Victory notes and what followed the announcer's voice saying, '*Ici Londres*'. It was a great morale-booster to the frustrated French people, and now in Antoine's house we were part of it. That night we sampled some of the wine in his cellar kept for special occasions.

I suppose we expected the call to come within one or two days, but it wasn't to be and we began to slip back into our normal daily

routine, although the radio watch was being kept faithfully. All sorts
of things which could have gone wrong went floating through my
mind and I became a wee bit disconsolate. Matters were made
worse, when one day I heard a tremendous commotion in the
passage outside my room which did not die down for some time.
Then Judith appeared, white-faced, to tell me in a whisper that
Fabien had had an accident at the factory and had lost his right
thumb. For a few days there were countless visitors, both family and
medical, together with the odd gendarme and factory official, which
proved a strain on both the family and myself; secrecy and silence on
my part were essential.

When all visitors had left, Fabien would join me in my room, I
think it helped him a great deal to share his pain and unhappiness
with me. We gave up the language lessons to play cards and
draughts. He even learnt to deal single-handed. Antoine used to join
us occasionally and bring in a bottle of wine, sometimes some of his
own home made stuff. He had developed the knack of making cider
too, a dangerous hobby as it happened. Shortly after going to bed one
night there was a tremendous explosion, or so it seemed, and the
whole family turned out in their night clothes expecting at least a
bombing raid. After a brief look outside, Antoine went straight to the
cellar to emerge after a few moments shaking with laughter. He had
placed his new batch of cider in a large container but, as was now
obvious, before it had ceased fermenting. The cellar was awash with
the remains of the cider and we all laid to with cloths, buckets and
mops to clear it up.

Antoine took me aside later to say that his first thought was that
some of his cache of arms had exploded, and we made a second trip
down to the cellar so that he could show me the place behind which
the arms were stored. None of the family knew about it, but he said
that he felt that he must confide in me, as we were both fighting men,
and I was like a son to him. I felt strangely honoured but also
alarmed that I was now mentally carrying about information which
could, if I were captured later and made to speak, lead not just to his
arrest but to his immediate execution.

It was shortly after this that I was given further information to
commit to memory by Edouard who made a special visit to Antoine's
to give me details of the whereabouts of a half dozen secret factories
and underground arsenals in the area which I could pass on if and
when I reached England. He was of the opinion that I would soon be

moving and as it happened he must have had his ear well to the ground.

Two mornings later, about six o'clock I was woken by Antoine, eyes wild with excitement.

'Herbert,' he whispered, '*nous avons "Très bien pour chocolat" par le radio. Levez-vous.*' I shot out of bed, washed myself in the large china bowl on the washstand and dressed myself in the clothes in which I had arrived, neatly folding those of Fabien's I had been using. Judith was already in the back room and had coffee and hot bread waiting for me. I ate and drank in a daze trying to collect my thoughts. Antoine patiently waited whilst I finished my meal, gently tapping his finger on the table. There was obviously no time to lose so I hurriedly swallowed the rest of the bread and got up still chewing.

Judith was already behind me holding my short blue coat. I slipped into it and turned to see tears in her eyes. '*Le Bon Dieu vous bénisse,*' she said solemnly and kissed both my cheeks. I asked about Fabien and the younger Judith but Antoine held the door to the passage open and said that it was better that we left straight away. It was almost a month since I came in through that same passage, and now I was going back out to goodness knows what. I tried to express my thanks to them both but the words couldn't get past the lump in my throat. The stout old front door closed behind me cutting me off from a host of fond memories. Antoine and I looked up at the low dripping clouds, turned up our coat collars and took the road into town.

Fourmies was hardly awake although I noticed a number of lights in houses where people were either careless or indifferent. Rain was beginning to fall in sheets as we automatically increased our pace; my thoughts at that moment were on the daunting prospect of another day out in the open in soaking wet clothes. Curious how a month of coddling had reduced my resilience.

Antoine tapped my shoulder, bringing me out of my contemplation, and pointed across the road. There, much to my surprise, was the original café we had entered when we first arrived in Fourmies. The street doors were closed, in fact Antoine didn't even try them, making his way down a side passage where he discreetly knocked on a side window. A door opened immediately and we were ushered into a darkened room and then through to the familiar room in which I had last eaten sandwiches. The café owner and his wife welcomed us and we were led through into the main room of the café, taking one of the tables and draping our wet coats over the spare chairs.

Antoine ordered two large glasses of marc and smiled at me, '*Pour boire à notre santé*,' he said.

Yes, it was the time for toasts and when the marc came I raised my glass first. '*À votre famille, qui sera toujours ma deuxième famille.*' Antoine nodded his head ceremoniously, drank, and added his own toast. '*À Herbert, mon troisième fils*'. It was then I discovered that he had another son, Antoine, older than Fabien and already married living in a nearby market town. I wondered what he might think of the risks his parents had been taking.

We spent a while chatting in the fragmented fashion I had come to accept with Antoine more concerned as to whether I was wearing my warmest underclothing and whether my shoes were watertight.

Then draining the last of his marc Antoine looked at his watch, stood up and began putting on his coat. I followed suit and we made our way in reverse through the café with emotional farewells and wishes of good luck from the two good souls who had given me shelter. Outside it was growing light but it was still raining, although the wind had died down.

Antoine led me to the road and pointed to a figure standing by a large tree, some hundred yards further on. '*Votre guide*,' he explained.

He held me by both shoulders giving me a long long look. It could have been a tear or a drop of rain running down his face. Pulling me towards him he hugged me and kissed me on both cheeks, his stubble rough against the skin.

'*Bon tour*,' he said tenderly and disappeared into the side passage of the café.

Involuntarily I started to follow him because I had not said goodbye as I would have wished, but after a few steps I turned towards the figure in the distance. My heart was very heavy, but I felt that I had to move on.

As I drew closer to the tree the figure drew back behind it and it crossed my mind that maybe the curfew was still in operation and it was still necessary to take every precaution to travel unobserved. I moved closer to the houses and garden hedges lining the road hoping that no one else was around.

Coming level with the tree I heard a voice low and urgent mutter, '*Ici*'.

The figure had a cowl over most of the head and I strained my eyes in the half light to pick out the face within. It was my night for

**Above** Madame Judith Renaud (right) and her daughter Judith, with a young cousin, taken in about 1978 in the cottage next door to where I was hidden.

**Below** Nounou (Elizabeth Warnon), her mother and son. A photograph taken by Constance (Elizabeth Liegois) on my visit to Brussels in 1947, at the Rue Vanderhoeven where I was hidden.

**Above** At the Trocadero in occupied Paris, three Allied airmen (centre group) surround an unsuspecting Kriegsmarine officer.

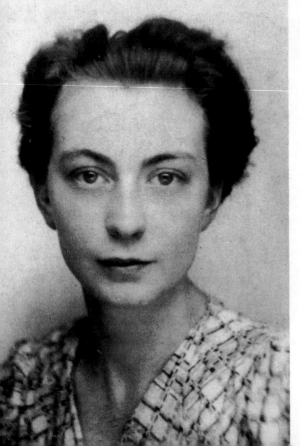

**Left** Andrée de Jongh.

surprises: the face was that of a pretty young girl who was now peering anxiously around me. Satisfied that there was no other persons in the area, she looked up and smiled sweetly. 'I am Emmeline; speak little English'.

The last statement was quite true, and I surmised that she had been given the job because of the few words that she had acquired. Offering me an oilskin cape she explained in both tongues but mainly French that we were going first to her father's farm a few miles away, where I would meet up again with some of the lads who had been with Madame Verdain. Never unhappy in the company of an attractive young lady, I set off with her with mounting anticipation of a successful 'run' home.

# CHAPTER EIGHT

# Brussels

My pretty little companion was no slouch when it came to walking and I found it increasingly hard to keep up with her, the oilskin cape was more a hindrance than a help although it did keep the rain out. Every so often Emmeline would look back, see that I was lagging, and stop to let me catch up. As a supposedly fit young man, I could not help feeling put out that a slip of a girl could easily outdistance me. We kept on the same road in torrential rain, occasionally being passed in the opposite direction by people presumably making their way into Fourmies. On every occasion this happened, Emmeline slipped her hand in mine which I felt was overdoing matters especially in that weather, but like Marguerite before her, she probably did it to avoid the slightest suspicion.

At the top of a rise in the road Emmeline suddenly pulled me off to the left onto a small path leading to a wood and within minutes we were moving in much drier conditions, although the rain was seeping through the trees here and there. We skirted what looked to be a small lake but there was little chance to enjoy the scenery in the damp gloom. Once again all that could be heard was the sucking sound of our shoes as we pulled them out of the leaves and mud underfoot. I stumbled now and then much to the amusement of Emmeline and she encouraged me with assurances that we were nearly at our destination. The condensation inside the cape was almost as bad as the dampness without and I was decidedly miserable, but the thought that I would soon see some of the French lads again kept me plodding on!

It came as quite a relief when Emmeline stopped me by placing one hand on my chest and the other to her lips in a gesture of silence. She was peering ahead and I could make out the grey ribbon of a metalled road below us. Down we went to the roadside, apprehensive but unnecessarily so, as there was no sound except for falling rain. Quickly across the road we entered the wood beyond into even denser woodland and continued our plodding for at least a mile until we again broke out of the trees onto an unmade farm track.

Emmeline pointed up the track and said, '*Voilà*, we arrive'. I felt definitely out of condition and ready for a rest!

The cart track was deep in mud and I lost a shoe twice before we sighted a tall building which turned out to be one of the hay barns of the farm owned by Emmeline's father. Emmeline finally stopped outside the double doors and motioned me to enter. A subdued roar of greeting met my ears and I could see all around me perched on parts of the barn, or in the hay, at least ten of Madame Verdain's brood, including André and Marc.

Emmeline went off saying that she would be back soon and I spent the next half hour sharing experiences with my former fellow travellers. Apparently the rest of the lads were being taken on another route by a Resistance group with contacts in Vichy France, there being too many to be handled by one group alone. Six of those I spoke to had been lodged with separate families, but the rest including André and Marc had stayed in this very barn since arriving at Fourmies and had, in fact, helped discreetly with some of the farm work.

Our gossip was cut short by the arrival of Emmeline, now visibly a petite curly-haired brunette, and her parents, stocky, red-faced and grey-haired carrying bread and hot milk. I was also given a heavy shirt, trousers and socks to change into whilst my own clothes were dried. The bread and milk were delicious and very soporific, it wasn't long before I slipped down into the hay for a refreshing sleep. A rolled up shirt thumping into my head soon brought me round and I awoke to find the inmates playing an impromptu game of football using the shirt as a ball.

'Wake up!' laughed André, throwing me a communal towel. 'The rain has stopped. Wash outside.'

Scratching my head I went off to find the large trough by a free standing tap which the lads had used for their ablutions. Primitive but practical, it served to freshen me up quickly.

Emmeline came back about midday with my dried clothes and bread and cheese for all. She gathered us together in the barn to explain that we would be leaving as soon as darkness fell to cross the border back into Belgium, where we would contact the group who would be waiting to take us on to the next stage. It would take about two hours and we needed to be wearing the warmest clothing we had and to have good shoes. Only one of the lads reported a hole in one of his shoes and Emmeline took his shoe size. Before leaving to find the shoes she said that we would be having a farewell meal before nightfall.

That last promise was well kept, as late in the afternoon, Emmeline and her family began to bring in closed tureens and other metal vessels, bottles of wine, bread and fruit. Then, lastly, her father arrived bearing a large dish with a metal cover, and lifting it to display a roasted piglet amid loud murmurs of delight. In view of the restrictions on the populace it was an impossible meal to have, but we settled down to it with much merriment and gastronomic joy. The family made sure that none of us drank too much wine but other than that we were able to eat to our hearts' content.

An hour passed of pure conviviality, with Emmeline being subjected to atrocious flirting by all the young males including myself, but she was more than a match for any of us and had a wider eye on her responsibilities that night. She finally took a long look at her watch, held up her hands and told us to get ready to move. We put on our outer clothes good-naturedly and slowly filed past Emmeline's father and mother expressing our gratitude for their help. Their solid country faces were lit up with delight and as we kissed each other's cheeks there was a suggestion of a tear or two even from the 'old soldier' who in his own way was serving France that night. Outside the barn Emmeline was marshalling the lads into single file, with myself immediately behind her and André and Marc following with the rest. Rain began to fall again as we moved off.

We retraced our steps along the cart track which was even more a morass than when we last took it. As I had done previously, some of the lads began to lose their shoes in the mud and I thanked heaven that I had tied two loops of thick twine around mine before we left the barn. My previous experience paid off handsomely. At the point where Emmeline and I had emerged from the wood earlier, she struck off in a different direction skirting the wood this time. It was quiet and dark, with no moon, rain falling almost vertically. The column of figures was producing a kind of hushed rustling sound, as we moved as silently as we could.

Emmeline turned after a while and motioned to me to turn left into the wood; the soundless message passed from me to the rear of the struggling line. Once again the going was extremely rough; muted curses could be heard as one or other of the lads stumbled into a tree trunk or matted undergrowth. Emmeline was walking quite confidently as if she had a miner's lamp on her rain hat; she obviously knew every inch of the way. It was just as well because there was no way of telling where we were without her. It began to get a little more solid underfoot and just faintly on our right we could see a lighter strip of land.

We paused on the top of an embankment and there below us was a double railway line. Emmeline whispered that it was the line to Momignies, the one we had crossed on our way in a month ago. Almost on tip-toe we made our way across the track and plunged into the safety of the next wood. There was more hard slogging to come, as the ground seemed to be much softer and marshy, and tiredness was already beginning to creep into my legs when we broke from the wood onto a path running alongside a very large body of water. Emmeline turned away to the left and we skirted the water for a good mile or so. Then back in the wood for a short period before Emmeline stopped us and whispered that we were on Belgian soil, but we had an hour or so yet of hard walking.

She wasn't kidding, but none of the young men behind her was going to be outpaced by a girl and much personal pride was disguised amongst the soft cries of complaint that we had not had a rest. Emmeline whispered that we had no time to rest, and straightaway pushed on, a living example of determined leadership. The disgruntled column got into line and lurched on!

You can imagine our relief when the trees eventually ended and we stood on sloping ground with a grey strip of tarmac below us, indicating a road to somewhere. The rain had mercifully stopped. Emmeline guided us down and along the side of the road until we reached a crossroad where she ordered us to lay hidden in a ditch for a short while. The ground was wet but so were our clothes, so there was no sense of discomfort. She finally appeared, to round us up and to hurry us straight across the junction. Some ten minutes more walking brought us to a farm track, as muddy as the one on her father's farm. Sloshing our way up this we arrived at a long low white farmhouse with a large oak door.

Emmeline knocked and a face appeared at a window, then bolts withdrew and we were ushered into a huge and gloriously warm kitchen and the presence of Madame Bachelart, an imposing Belgian lady, much like a larger edition of Madame Verdain, with the same authoritative voice and air of dominance over her environment. Behind all that was a kind and humorous person as we were to discover. Under her guidance we males disrobed down to our underclothes and spread them around on various clothes horses and cane chairs. Emmeline went off to be separately looked after. Before long we were seated at the long wooden table in the kitchen, wolfing down hot meaty soup and farmhouse bread. Good strong coffee produced complete euphoria and the room was filled with happy babblers, interrupted only when Emmeline appeared, amid cheers and thanksgiving. Madame Bachelart bustled around the whole time serving and joining in the banter, which was more from relief than anything else.

Like all good parties it had to come to an end and Emmeline, who had changed her clothing, came to each of us individually and said her goodbyes. She was returning immediately to her father's farm, the same way as she had come, but this time alone. I never asked but I suppose she picked up her other clothes next time round.

'Goodbye,' she said to me as we kissed cheeks. 'See you again.'

She had found some perfume from somewhere, mixing her femininity with her undoubted bravado. Quite a character and a pretty one. If circumstances permitted after the war I would certainly try to see her again.

There was little time after she had left to revive the jollity. Some half an hour afterwards Madame Bachelart ushered in two ladies in their early thirties and introduced them as Constance and Nounou. They were members of the Comète escape line and had come for me, and me only. Constance looked the elder of the two but this was probably because of her severe style of dress, a brown jacket and skirt, trilby style hat and heavy shoes. She was by no means ugly but in contrast with Nounou's obvious femininity she was almost mannish, with no make-up and her rich brown hair tucked up under the hat. Nounou, on the other hand, obviously enjoyed colour in her clothes and make-up and she made the most of her elfin face with its sharply pointed chin, and her long blonde hair. One thing they shared in common was an air of complete assurance and I instantly felt that I was under professional care.

It was a disappointment that none of the lads would be coming with me, when I asked about them I was given a polite reply, 'Perhaps later.' Apologetically I made my farewells to the lads, but they quite understood.

'See you in London,' said André.

'Yes,' confirmed Marc. '*Vive de Gaulle.*'

It took but a moment to put the rest of my clothes on and after a brief goodbye from Madame Bachelart, we three were back out in the dark heading towards the railway station, first having to pick our way down the execrable farm track. Surprisingly it was not far to the station and Nounou and I stayed in the shadow of the forecourt whilst Constance went to buy my ticket. She emerged shortly afterwards and we made our way onto the platform without being challenged. The train was not due for ten minutes so we hurried along to a small shelter. I smiled as I saw the 'Momignies' sign under a lamp; a good month had gone by since last time, but I certainly wouldn't forget that name.

Seated on a rough bench between the two ladies I asked after a few minutes where we were going. 'Brussels,' whispered Constance then, 'Say nothing more.' Ah well, it looked as if we were back to the deaf and dumb routine again!

We were quickly off the bench as the train roared in but it continued on its way without stopping which was just as well, being filled with German troops; another reminder how dangerous this business was. Our own train followed in behind and kept up a sedate pace thereafter, with us comfortably installed on one side of a twelve seat compartment. Again I was seated between the two ladies in complete isolation from the other passengers. Feigning sleep came naturally, in fact I did slip away once or twice, due, I expect, to the exertions of the walk with Emmeline, but each time was gently brought back by Nounou's elbow. It was obviously a time for concentration and alertness. The only large town we stopped at was Charleroi, also filled with occupying troops on the move but fortunately none chose our compartment. The journey was getting to be a bit of a drag and I passed the time running through in my mind the various French songs and phrases that I had learnt. At a pinch I reckoned I could cope with most situations, if ever I was left on my own. This was hardly likely though now that I was in the hands of an expert organisation. I looked at the calm faces on either side of me and thanked my lucky stars!

Buildings began to show on the skyline in growing profusion, heralding the advent of a large city, and minute by minute we drew deeper into the heart of Brussels. At long last the train jolted to a halt and we got down onto a dimly lit platform. Constance pulled me to one side and whispered:

'You go with Nounou like sweethearts. Yes!'

Nounou grabbed my arm and pulled me along, looking up at me with large loving eyes and gabbling away incessantly. Through the ticket barrier and into a main foyer with Nounou skipping beside me and laughing. Suddenly she stopped and gave me a big kiss and I entered into the spirit of things wholeheartedly!

In this vein we passed across the foyer into the main street beyond where we stopped to wait for Constance. Nounou smiled at me. 'Good', she laughed. 'Many police and Gestapo there.'

Constance joined us shortly after and we made our way to a tram terminus. Once I had got used to the strident noise of the bell push operated by the morose conductor I settled down to the ride which was not to be a straightforward one. In face we changed twice in quick succession and I wondered whether we were throwing someone off the scent, only to discover later that the journey from the Station we arrived at required three trams. On the whole, the Belgian civilians in the trams seemed a lot less sad than their French counterparts in Paris and more healthy. The last tram we caught lumbered along stopping almost everywhere and finally came to rest in a big open square. From here we walked hurriedly through a number of streets until we reached a wide avenue, the Chaussée de Louvain and after turning onto this for a few minutes we slipped into a small side street and stood before the street door of a three-storeyed building. A swift check up and down the street by Constance ended in a nod to Nounou who let us into the building.

We were welcomed in the hallway by Nounou's mother, a petite lady in black, and led into the salon where hot coffee and sandwiches were waiting on a large square table covered with a thick lace cloth. After the long travels the food was more than welcome and I tucked in while the two women went over their adventures with Nounou's mother. The salon was very similar to the one in Marguerite's parents' flat in Paris, although the Belgian furniture was much heavier and less elegant. Several china cabinets lined the walls, their rich dark wood blending well with the thick rugs and curtains. The three ladies sat cosily around the fireplace, momentarily forgetting my existence. I made an obvious noise with my empty cup, immediately attracting Nounou's attention. 'Come,' she said, 'you must to be tired', and ushered me from the salon as Constance called out, 'Sleep well.'

Just past the salon door was a descending staircase and we made our way in half darkness to the landing below. A door opened off this into a well lit room filled with tobacco smoke and several men sitting around on camp beds and an occasional chair. Nounou smiling addressed the assembly: '*Je vous présente Herbert, un anglais*', and pointed to an empty bed in one corner. 'That is for you.'

I threw my haversack onto it and spent the next few minutes shaking hands and meeting my new room mates, four in all. One was a middle-aged Belgian doctor who was addressed throughout as '*Monsieur le Docteur*', next a young French army captain called Yves, then Lucien a dour Belgian Walloon whom I suspected was there solely as a listener and lastly a Polish nobleman and officer André de Visigota, tall, elegant even in shabby clothes and speaking fluent French and English. A motley crowd but all seeking passage to England for their own reasons.

Yves and André were the more interested in my story and we sat on my bed as I brought them up to date as best as I could without naming names or areas. Yves was an explosives expert hoping to join de Gaulle and André was a fugitive from Poland also hoping to join his country's forces in England. After a few cigarettes, I intimated that I was ready for bed and they courteously withdrew while I put on the pyjamas in my haversack, none the worse for their journey and quite dry. For a while there was desultory conversation between the other occupants but one by one they each took to their beds and I was able to drift off into a glorious sleep.

Morning brought with it a burst of feverish activity as my companions jostled to use the small sink or washing basin in the corner of the room. There were muffled comments about the tepid water coming from the hot tap but one by one each managed to wash and shave except for Yves who sported a smart, pointed beard. Rising last I was in the middle of my ablutions when Nounou came in carrying coffee and warm rolls. She called over to me to have my breakfast and to come upstairs to the salon.

My appetite made short work of breakfast and tidying myself up I left the room amid joking remarks from the others that I was more favoured and about to jump the queue. Mounting the stairs with some eagerness, I had almost convinced myself that my companions were right when I arrived at the salon door. Nounou must have been waiting, for the door swung open and she pointed to an empty chair by the table. Constance was peering round the heavy curtains covering the window to the street, almost as if expecting visitors. But with some surprise I realised that the visitors were already in the room, two men in smart raincoats quietly conversing with Nounou's mother. They looked over as I sat down and after a few moments moved towards the table carrying their chairs. There were no introductions, their pallid faces crowned with neatly groomed hair showed no signs of pleasantness or humour. You instantly felt that you were in the presence of men who were capable of any act of violence towards you yet who were in some strange way also ready to give you their assistance providing they could accept you as genuine.

To say that I felt uneasy would be an understatement; my previous interrogation in Paris had been extremely searching but this one had to be right or I could be a goner. Much of the questioning followed the Paris pattern but whereas I had not been forthcoming in Paris about the details of the bombing operations and service details, I decided to give these gentlemen any detail asked. And there were plenty of questions, all in good English, shared alternately by each of them. Apprehension was beginning to make my clothes feel clammy and I shot up in my chair when both men suddenly stood up and walked back to the glowing fireplace. They stood in quiet consultation with the three ladies and then one came over to me actually smiling and offering me his hand.

'I think we can help you,' he said.

His companion joined us and also shook my hand, but unsmiling: '*Au revoir*,' he murmured.

Without further ado both men swept from the room and the ladies came forward to welcome me into the fold officially. I was later to find out that only weeks previously several of the group had been arrested through infiltration of the organisation by two Germans posing as English airmen. No wonder they were being so extra careful!

We sat drinking coffee as Constance and Nounou explained the next steps to be taken. Apparently all had agreed that my wide face and rosy complexion would allow me to pose successfully as a young Dutchman and that arrangements would now be made for the necessary papers, clothing and incidentals to be obtained and prepared. Until then I must pass the time with my four companions down below, hopefully for not more than a week. I returned downstairs hardly crestfallen but still a little impatient to get on with the next part of the adventure, for adventure it certainly was, and I paid little heed to the enormous risks that were being taken on my behalf.

In our basement room we passed the days smoking, reading anything that came to hand, playing all manner of card games without knowing the rules properly, having our meals and generally chatting about our earlier lives rather than the circumstances that brought about our predicament. Lucien had little to pass on, if he was a friendly informer, and he tended to keep to himself until the day came when Constance provided us with a tiddleywink set. Lucien was fascinated by it and was instrumental in setting up an international series of games in which France, Belgium, England, Holland and Poland took part. The series extended over three days with Lucien representing Holland since he was half Dutch anyway and countless games were involved. Suffice it to say that England and Holland fought out an exciting final with England victorious by a tiddle, or maybe a wink!!

During this time one or other of us was occasionally called upstairs for some purpose or other, to which we never referred, and on one occasion I was introduced in the salon to a pleasant rotund and balding little man who spent a half hour reshaping my hair into a traditional Dutch style rather reminiscent of the 'pudding basin' style which was rife in my childhood, where the hair was trimmed to a line halfway up the head all round. My companions spent a few hours cracking jokes about that.

My next trip upstairs was to meet a tall, grey-haired tailor who took all the traditional measurements and returned the next day for a fitting, using a brick-coloured cloth which I thought a little loud for my taste but thought it wiser not to press the matter. Two more days passed and I was back upstairs actually trying the suit on and I must say that I was more than a little impressed with the finished article which had a natty line and a half belt in the back of the jacket. My only criticism was the use of a dull black material as a lining, not only of the coat but of the trousers too, but presumably this was how the Dutch did it, so I had to put up with it.

Came the day when I was again in the salon with Constance and Nounou who explained that we were going out. Quite a bombshell that. Was I to put on my new suit? No, I was to wear what I had arrived in. I felt that some problem had arisen but they were both smiling so I went below to get my short jacket. Constance and Nounou were waiting in the hall as I arrived back and we all three emerged into Brussels in daylight with all its city smells and noises. The streets were crowded and shepherded between both ladies I took in as many of the sights as I could. German troops were everywhere, even on the trams we rode in, but the air of oppression did nothing to dampen the magnificence of the buildings and the prettiness of the parks and gardens. A kaleidoscope of impressions were compressed into a very short time and as if by magic we turned a corner into a wide avenue filled with departmental stores. Entering one we took an escalator to an upper floor and after passing through a couple of clothing departments came to a halt in front of an automatic photo machine similar to those used for passports. A queue of a dozen or so were waiting and immediately in front of us was a young German soldier and his girl friend, obviously wanting a souvenir of their relationship. Constance stood waiting whilst Nounou and I moved forward in our turn, whilst other people queued behind us including more German soldiery.

Nounou leaned forward and whispered in my ear, 'For your papers.'

I was amazed at her calm courage. Before long we were inside the photo cabin and Nounou and I sat on the hard round seats provided.

'No smile,' she hissed.

The machine clicked and we were out again pushing our way through shoppers to the road outside. I stayed with Constance whilst Nounou went back in to get the photos which the machine had by that time disgorged. She returned after a brief while with a nod of success and a grin.

The way back to the Rue Vanderhoeven was quick and direct. My female protectors obviously did not want to expose me to any more danger than was necessary. It did occur to me that if the Gestapo were aware that British Servicemen were being ferried out of Europe with false papers, surely they would guess that photo machines would be of value to those producing the papers. Maybe the quick route home was another safety precaution in case someone had been watching for suspicious users of the machine. Indoors both Nounou and Constance showed clear signs of relief that we had come to no harm.

Two more days ensued before I was again summoned aloft to meet the more pleasant one of my previous interrogators. He had brought the finished identity card with the thrilling news that I would be leaving the following evening by train for Paris in his company. We would be travelling first class and I would take a corner seat in the same carriage as he, but he would take the opposite diagonal corner seat. There would be at least two control points where papers would be inspected and at no stage would I indicate that we were known to each other. In the event of difficulties I was to answer any questions in Dutch-sounding gibberish, as most Germans and others couldn't get on with the Dutch language and it was the safest one for impostors to use. At the station he would hand me an '*Ausweiss*' which was in the process of being prepared which would permit me as a Dutch student to return to Bayonne via Paris to continue studies in agriculture. I flipped open the identity card and saw the photo we had obtained in the department store. It looked incredibly genuine with one corner partly obscured by the issuing authorities stamp, and some slight wear on another corner. Whoever had done it had been very careful to make it seem authentic. My name was Wim Breendonck from Eindhoven, a student; aged 21. Perfect!

Nounou handed me my new suit with a thick shirt and tie to go with it, and a flat pork pie hat, also an overnight bag.

'Your shoes are OK,' she confirmed. 'Rest all you can.'

I shook hands with my new guide to be and went back to the basement room carrying my spoils. There was more excitement down below, Monsieur le Docteur had also been told he was leaving for Paris, but with a different guide. André had volunteered to stay with the organisation and would be acting much as Nounou and Constance were doing, bringing in Allied servicemen and other evaders who were wanting help to get to England. Yves and Lucien had to bide their time, but they put a brave face on things and joined in the general hubbub of celebration. André who had always nurtured a longing for my pullover finally persuaded me to exchange it for a neat grey overcoat with a black velvet collar which I thought rounded off my new image.

Sleep was almost impossible that night as I lay on my camp bed and pondered over the chances of making it to England. The Comète organisation was so professional in its attitude that it inspired confidence from the start. Even the smallest detail seemed to be covered, down to the Dutch cigarettes and odd coins in my new jacket pocket. Travelling first class was another example of their colossal cheek in all that they did. From their experience, Germans were always impressed with authority and superiority and naturally treated first class passengers more leniently, and it was far more possible to avoid searching questions at control points. There appeared to be little to worry about; I rolled over at last, and nodded off.

By the time I awoke I had missed breakfast by hours and my companions were already busy at cards. Washing and shaving in leisurely fashion I mused on the fact that if all went well I would be in Spain in three days; maybe for Christmas. There was a lot to come before that though and much would depend on the strength of the Comète line.

'Come and take a hand,' called André, cutting through my thoughts. My wave of dismissal of the idea brought cries of disapproval from the players but André understood. He came over to my bed grinning. 'Nervous? he asked.

'Not half,' I replied. 'How about giving me some idea of what Dutch sounds like?' We spent the rest of that morning practising nonsense phrases which had a ring of authenticity in them.

Nounou arrived with sandwiches and coffee just after midday but these were for Yves, Lucien and André. Monsieur le Docteur and I were invited up to the salon for a huge cooked meal as it was likely that we would not get anything that night in Paris. Nervous anticipation had not killed our appetites and we ate well whilst we tried to squeeze information about our journey from our lady hostesses. We might as well not have tried. Constance and Nounou had been too long in the game to allow us to know too many details in advance. They just smiled and shook their heads.

Lunch over, they said, 'Rest as much as you can. Be dressed at five o'clock.' A replete Monsieur le Docteur and I descended again into our 'hidey hole' and flung ourselves on our beds despite repeated demands from our companions to join in their pastimes.

We were both dressed well before five o'clock with our overnight bags packed and struggling to get a view of ourselves in the small mirror on the wall above the wash bowl.

'More like pimps than anything,' chortled André, 'but I suppose you'll pass in a crowd.' Monsieur le Docteur looked quite distinguished in a charcoal grey suit and I took heart that I must look similarly acceptable.

Constance entered the room amid banter and gave us both the once-over, making the usual female finishing touches to our ties and collars. '*En avant!*' she barked. 'Let's go.'

Upstairs Nounou was already dressed for going out and there was a younger woman with her, small and vivacious with dark hair drawn over one eye. Again, no introductions, and as soon as Constance and Nounou's mother had said their goodbyes, the young woman grabbed Monsieur le Docteur's arm and steered him out into the street.

Nounou looked at me. 'Now it begins,' she said and took my arm. A last kiss on the cheeks from the two ladies I was leaving behind and we were out and walking rapidly to the tram stop. There was no sign of the other two.

The journey to the main station in Brussels despite the three changes took no time at all, or so it seemed in my state of heightened emotion. Like all termini it was crawling with travellers but I remembered Nounou's remarks about the Gestapo when I had first arrived in Brussels, and this kept my adrenalin flowing. Evening was approaching and we reached the steps up to the main foyer, my male guide appeared, shook hands quickly and passed me the permit and the train ticket.

I felt a touch on my cheek; Nounou was smiling. '*Au revoir, Herbert,*' she whispered.

As she walked off I could see her swinging her shoulder bag as if in defiance of her country's oppressors.

CHAPTER NINE

# To Paris and Beyond

My companion coughed and pointed up the steps to the main foyer. Turning away from the receding view of Nounou with some sadness I nodded gravely and we both mounted the steps, quickly becoming absorbed in the moving mass of people finding their various trains. The Paris train was already waiting at its platform and I followed my silent guide through the barrier offering my ticket as nonchalantly as I could. The official and his attendant policeman hardly gave me a look. Duly heartened I kept my guide in view and entered the same carriage door. He was in the corridor and as I drew level he indicated the seat I should take. Some sort of businessman was already reading a newspaper in one of the seats, so completely engrossed that he did not raise his head. I chucked the overnight bag onto the luggage rack and settled in the corner. After some minutes my guide eased his way past to his own place.

Not knowing the time of departure put me at a disadvantage but there was plenty of activity outside and it looked as if we were moving off soon. This was more or less confirmed as in quick succession the other three seats were filled by well dressed civilians. We played the usual travellers' game of sizing each other up but I quickly feigned a lack of interest and sat idly watching the antics on the platform. My thoughts bordered on amusement wondering what these gentlemen would say if they knew the truth. It mattered not, a high whistle sounded and we were on our way to Paris, if our luck held.

The gentle rocking of the train was hardly noticeable in the deep recesses of the plush carriage seats. Once again I found myself running over my French vocabulary, and the nonsense phrases I had learnt with André de Visigota, wondering if I would have to put them to use. A ticket inspector looked in at one stage to check our tickets again, but it was a mere formality for which he deeply apologised. A better test was to come as we slowed down to a halt at the first control point.

It took some time before the carriage door opened to admit a helmeted German soldier demanding, '*Papieren*' in a subdued voice. So it does work, I thought, and offered my permit and identity card in casual fashion, although to be fair I was quaking a little inside. Two looks up and down by the grim face under the helmet and I was greatly relieved to hear his polite '*Danke*' as he returned the documents. One of the men opposite was asked a question which I could not hear, but apart from that the check went smoothly. I had the urge to look at my guide and smile, but I killed it quickly.

The second control point was even less a problem, only the scantiest glance being given to any of the documents offered, and I began to breathe more easily. My estimation of the organisation rose to the highest heights and I sat amazed at the simplicity of it all, yet much depended on luck despite the quality of the documents and the guides provided. Dwelling on the goodness of all the people I had met so far, I reverted to my usual snooze position for the rest of the journey and waited for the next test at the barrier in Paris.

Apart from my guide a guardian angel must have been with us, because we went through the barrier without a murmur, although one or two people were being stopped for questioning. There was no point in hanging about and we quickly threaded through the jostling throng to find our way to the nearest Metro station. Paris lay under dull dripping cloud but even though it was dark it looked beautiful to me, almost as if I was back home. Much had happened since I left here with Madame Verdain. Scurrying down the Metro stairs we were lucky to board a train straightaway, and after another change of trains we emerged in a quiet tree lined area with not many people about.

We stopped in the middle of the road that ran past the Metro station for a cautious look for any followers but everything seemed quiet. Opposite lay a block of flats and we made our way quickly inside. The lift was not working but we had only five floors to climb before we reached our destination. Three double raps on one of the flat doors produced the appearance of a well built man in a singlet and trousers with a mop of curly hair and moustache to match. He smiled broadly as my guide quietly greeted him with, '*Bonsoir, Aimable.*'

I was shown through to a bedroom with a huge bed in it and my guide shook hands with me and disappeared after a brief word with Aimable. So far so good!

Aimable spoke French only but he explained slowly that I would sleep there the night and move on the next day, in the company of Dédée, the leader of the organisation. He knew, or said he knew, no more, and though he produced coffee and some bread and cheese and we sat and chatted in general about the trip from Brussels, I was no wiser at the end. Once again I was shoved off to bed with advice to get as much rest as possible. Little did I know what for.

Paris was its usual noisy self in the morning and I woke up fighting fit, finding my way into the adjoining bathroom for a welcome soak and general clean up. Aimable appeared shortly afterwards with coffee and rolls with a rare treat of jam, fruit unrecognised. He was off to work but I would have a visitor in an hour or two. Probably this Dédée he was talking about. A Paris newspaper had been left in the kitchen and I passed the time away trying to do the crossword. It occurred to me after a while that I had disobeyed orders for the first time in leaving the bedroom to visit the kitchen. Aimable had been very insistent that I should stay quiet and in one room. After returning the newspaper I lay on the bed mulling over my progress: it was nearly two months since I had parachuted. Hopefully my note which I wrote in Fourmies might have reached my parents, but if not there was every possibility now that the organisation had informed London that they had picked me up. I decided to ask this Dédée about it when he appeared.

As if on cue there was a tap on the bedroom door and in came my guide who had brought me from Brussels. Behind him a slighter figure with fresh face and curly hair, looking round the room with interest. 'Sergeant Smith, Canadian flyer,' said my guide by way of introduction; so he spoke some English! He addressed us both very briefly. 'Stay here. I will come back later.'

The new arrival looked a bit nonplussed until I broke the ice. 'Bert Spiller, RAF observer,' I explained offering my hand. We shook hands solemnly but no more was said for several minutes during which the Canadian slowly ambled round the room taking in the surroundings.

I found it extremely hard to formulate sentences in English after having acclimatised myself to French, and eventually blurted out, 'Have you been in France long? I'm sorry, I'm finding English very strange after the last two months.'

The Canadian nodded. 'Me too, I've been down since late October.'

He came across to the large bed and lay down. 'Boy, this is better than the crummy joint I've been in for weeks.'

Slowly we began to put our conversation together, but I was conscious that Smitty as I came to call him was not fully convinced that he was in friendly hands. He couldn't be drawn on any of the details of his last operation or squadron apart from the fact that he had been piloting a stricken Wellington and had excaped by parachute. Like me he had not seen any of his crew, but had been brought in quickly to Paris after having been picked up within minutes by a Resistance group. Since then he had been 'going the rounds' or moving from one safe house to another until finally Comète had got to hear of him. He listened carefully to my story as if waiting to pick holes in it, even asking questions about my own ill-fated operation, and eventually seemed satisfied enough to drop off to sleep. In view of my previous advice I was content to let him catch up on any missed sleep, and lay on the other side of the bed in ruminative silence.

It wasn't long though before my Brussels guide was back but this time with a very welcome middle-aged lady unusually dressed in light blue, not the customary black, carrying a cloth-covered tray, which she placed on the dressing table. Smitty wasn't very happy about being woken up but when he smelt the coffee and hot bread he changed his mind. There was a good cheese too and an apple apiece.

'*Bon appétit*,' smiled the lady, backing out of the room. My guide left shortly afterwards, after informing us that Dédée would see us within the hour.

Lunch over, Smitty was quick to 'hit the sack' again and sprawled across the bed in disarray. I lay for a while admiring my identity card and *Ausweiss* and wondered what Smitty was carrying; he hadn't produced anything. He had discovered one thing though – that the Dédée we kept hearing about was a woman and not a man as I had previously thought. Boy, she must be some sort of Valkyrie to run a successful and professional organisation like this. I must have dozed off because we were both caught completely by surprise by my guide waggling our feet to wake us up.

'Dédée will see you in the salon,' he urged. We jumped up and hastily tidied up our clothes.

Entering the salon with some trepidation we were astonished to see an attractive young woman, not a classic beauty but nevertheless fresh and vibrant. Her slim figure dressed in a simple blouse and skirt made her look like a teenager and her short bobbed hair and clear eager blue eyes did the same. 'Hallo,' she greeted us, 'I am Dédée'. She shook our hands with a wide smile and with a wave of her hand towards the table said, 'Please sit down.'

The immediate impression was that here was someone very much in charge whose instructions were explicit and were to be followed without question. They came thick and fast. We would be travelling that evening on the express to Bayonne, sleeping overnight on the train to reach Bayonne in the early morning. Travel would again be first class with Smitty and I in opposite corners with Dédée in the other corner seat on Smitty's side. We would be staying overnight near Bayonne and would, if all went well, be making a crossing over the Pyrenees the following night. It would also be necessary at one point to ride bicycles; we both confirmed that there would be no problem. We would not be the only ones to be making the journey over the Pyrenees, there would be others who might be known to us. Monsieur le Docteur perhaps, I thought.

Dédée then inspected our papers and our clothing and expressed satisfaction except for my pork pie hat which was discarded. We each had a few French banknotes to put in our pockets and finally the rail tickets for Bayonne.

'Good,' Dédée finally exclaimed. 'I'll see you in three hours.' Suddenly she was gone, but the air still seemed to be charged with her personality. No wonder she was called the 'Little Cyclone' at times.

'Some girl eh?' murmured Smitty from his now customary position on the big bed. 'Do you think she'll do the whole trip with us?'

I couldn't see why not; she had that special driving force that champions have, and I was very glad that she was not only on my side, but also at my side, when it mattered.

'Why not?' I replied. 'She's strong enough for all of us.'

Smitty rolled over. 'Yep. I guess you're right,' he yawned.

We had been dozing for some time when our middle-aged lady friend was again ushered in with another tray. This time there were large bowls of thick meaty soup with huge chunks of bread, coffee and more apples.

'Eat well. You have a long way to go,' said my Brussels guide, quietly shepherding the lady from the room.

Smitty sat up and shrugged his shoulders. 'Well, let's go,' he commanded and we tucked in with relish. He spoke of Canada and that he would ask to go back there if he made it to England in one piece. He was still a little doubtful but some of my optimism was beginning to rub off. I told him that having got onto the conveyor belt there was little chance that the Comète organisation would fail now. Our conversation began to be liberally laced with joking banter and finally cemented the relationship and trust that we would need to make our home run successful.

No one came to clear away the tray and we were beginning to wonder whether some circumstance had arisen to cancel the journey that night. It was well over three hours since we had last seen Dédée, and our nervousness was mounting making any delay seem endless. We were distinctly relieved when the bedroom door opened to admit Dédée and the Brussels guide.

'OK,' she said. 'Get dressed. We go now.'

She had added a short thick coat and heavy walking shoes to what she had been wearing, an indication of what might lay before us.

Out in the cold air of the street I was glad of my overcoat; Smitty had to rely on the suit he had been given which was fortunately a fairly heavy tweed type. We did the Metro trip to the railway station in two pairs, using different carriages, Dédée and Smitty leading. The Bordeaux express, which terminated at Bayonne, was hissing quietly alongside its platform with the ticket inspector at the barrier flanked by attendant police. A queue of travellers were slowly moving forward as we approached.

Dédée stopped suddenly for a final word.

'Go through the barrier separately and enter the same carriage as me.'

The Brussels guide patted Smitty and me on our shoulders and quickly disappeared into the moving mass of travellers making for their trains. I had no time to wish him well or thank him for his efforts.

By the time I reached the queue for Bayonne Dédée was already several places up and Smitty was two in front of me. To me he looked extremely Anglo-Saxon and I fervently hoped he would get through without being stopped. Either the ticket inspector was under pressure, or the first class ticket routine scotched any enquiry, for we went through unnoticed in a very hurried fashion.

Looking ahead I could see Dédée further along the platform and so soon as she saw we had picked her out, she went forward into one of the carriages. In similar fashion to the trip from Brussels, Dédée was in the corridor to indicate which compartment we were to enter, and we both sank into our seats gratefully, for my part with my blood still racing from the nervous excitement of passing inspection at the barrier.

The train seemed to be popular enough and even when the rest of the seats in the compartment had been taken up, several people, mostly youngsters, filled up the corridor outside, sitting on their bags and rucksacks. For some reason it made you feel safer and part of the scenery, and our fellow travellers in the compartment were elderly and not likely to pry or find our presence suspicious. Enveloped in a self-induced aura of safety I fell back on my usual practice of appearing to doze and waited for the hours to go by. Smitty looked to be captivated by the pre-departure bustle going on outside, but Dédée was already leaning back with closed eyes. We finally got off to a smooth start and the outlines of Paris soon faded behind. Off again then on another step nearer to England, this time in the company of another very brave lady.

One of the elderly passengers fortunately asked Dédée to lower the blind across the window; asking Smitty might have been a little dangerous, although I am quite sure Dédée would have had some answer up her sleeve. To put off any similar request to me I quickly pulled down the smaller blind on my side. I felt that I was beginning to get the hang of this evasion business. Tucking my head into the soft corner of the seat I feigned a doze, keeping a listening watch for any sign of trouble. The train rattled on through the night with hardly a variance in its speed.

Twice I was surprised to find myself awaking from sleep to discover that officials were inspecting tickets and papers. No doubt my calmness in waking gave me the air of a genuine traveller, for apart from a brief glance at the documents I was proffering, the officials passed on without comment. Strangely enough, like an actor, I was beginning to live the part and felt quite comfortable in these stressful circumstances. When the man had gone the second time round I hazarded a look over towards Dédée's corner seat. A tiny smile lifted one corner of her mouth before she turned her head away, and I glowed with appreciation for her efforts and those of her organisation.

Amazingly nothing else happened to disturb our peace as we sped through the night and into the early morning to eventually make a stop at Bordeaux. The usual large groups of German servicemen were well in evidence on the platforms and these obviously were finding their way into the rear '*Nur für Wehrmacht*' carriages which had nearly cost me my freedom in St Dizier.

We were off again in a very short while to complete the final leg to Bayonne over increasingly beautiful countryside with distant views of the sea, bringing with it the welling up of all the hopes that had been latent within me for the last few weeks.

Drawing into the station at Bayonne the train gave a mighty whistle, which I could have echoed having got this far. It provided the signal for everyone to get ready to depart and in the general movement to assemble baggage and clothes Dédée pushed past into the corridor outside with Smitty faithfully behind her. I waited for one of the elderly couples to leave and then followed behind keeping Dédée and Smitty in sight. Another barrier was ahead but there was quite a crush of people and the two officials standing at the barrier were not going to check much; the tide swept on and within a few minutes we were outside in the street having offered nothing but our tickets for inspection.

Dédée moved along the street with Smitty and me in tow, both of us rubber-necking at the new surroundings as we went. We turned into a kind of promenade edged with light blue railings where we could see either the sea or an estuary to the left and a row of restaurants and cafés to the right. There were occasional public benches facing the water and Dédée eventually stopped at one of these, beckoning us to sit down. We hadn't long to wait before a slim man in his thirties wearing a beret at a rakish angle walked purposefully towards us.

'Hallo, chaps. Not a bad day eh?' he said in cultured tones, as he briefly shook hands with Dédée. He greeted her in French with an incredible English accent which I thought at the time would have betrayed him instantly to the German authorities, but he seemed quite at ease and most affable.

'I must leave you with B for a while,' explained Dédée. 'He will look after you.'

That was as much of an introduction as we were going to get, and we watched her retrace her steps back along the promenade with her springy confident style.

'How about a drink, chaps?' asked B. We were only too ready for that and he led us across the promenade to one of the cafés. Here he ordered three '*blondes*' beers in his terrible accent while Smitty and I sat in silence looking out on the distant waves. 'We're taking a bus to a friend's house nearby but we have half an hour yet,' whispered B. The old edgy feeling came creeping back, prompted I suppose by Dédée's absence, and the time passed very slowly as we occasionally sipped our beers.

At last B stood up and made ready to leave. '*En avant, suivez moi.*' The accent was almost comic. Hurrying from the café we wended our way through some side streets to a green painted metal bus shelter where several people were waiting. The bus was not long in coming and we took our seats under B.'s direction. I had a moment of consternation when B. appeared to say that we were three Englishmen to the conductor, but there was not the slightest response apart from the issue of three tickets. Later I learnt that our destination was the village of Anglet which had much the same sound as Anglais when pronounced.

The ride was interesting from a scenic point of view with occasional glimpses of distant mountains and blue sea. Though it was late December, the temperature was very comfortable and there was still some colour about in the fields and gardens we were passing. Anglet arrived too soon in one sense for I was enjoying the run, but we came to a jerky unceremonious halt and had to quickly follow B. as he made for the way out. We had some dusty roads to tread after that until we finally arrived at the entrance to a villa set back in its own grounds.

'This is it,' said B., 'Come in and meet Tante Go.'

The villa looked a little neglected as we approached it from the drive; the grey paintwork was beginning to peel off and the whole effect was drab. This couldn't however, be said of the lady who met us at the door. She had the same piercing eyes of Madame Verdain, but she was much slighter with reddish hair. Here again, you could sense authority and gritty determination, blended with a touch of overt feminism as she stood there in a pretty dress with light house shoes.

'Come, come. *Entrez!*' she ordered.

We filed in submissively and went through to a large lounge where an elderly lady awaited us. 'This is Bobonne, my mother,' Tante Go explained.

Smitty and I shook hands with Bobonne, a short plump lady with greying hair and a wide welcoming smile. 'And', interjected B., 'this is Tante Go who looks after this end of the Comète line.'

Tante Go raised her shoulders in a dismissive shrug and invited us to sit in the armchairs by the fireplace whilst coffee was prepared. Later, over coffee, Tante Go briefed us on the next stage of our journey. First we would have a hearty lunch because in all probability we would be crossing into Spain that night and we would need as much nourishment as we could get as the journey was arduous even for strong young men. Then we would leave the villa for the local railway station to take a local train to St Jean de Luz, a small fishing port. Outside the railway station at St Jean de Luz would be a number of bicycles which we would use to take us some way towards a farmhouse at the foot of the Pyrenees mountains, the remainder of the journey being on foot. At the farmhouse we would wait for the guide who would take us over the mountains. Dédée would be arriving soon at the villa and would escort us to the farmhouse and most probably into Spain.

Smitty and I blew out our cheeks in wonderment at the machine-like quality of the arrangements.

'You will be given the correct permits to travel in this area,' concluded Tante Go. 'We have an arrangement with the local German Kommandantur.' Her studied wink was explanation enough.

We sat until lunch time chatting generally with B. about England and Canada, with Tante Go as an occasional interested listener. B. would translate when she had difficulty with our idioms and jargon. Dédée timed her entry to the minute because as she arrived Bobonne came into the salon to say that lunch was ready. Smitty and I were certainly not ready in the expectant sense for the meal that awaited us for lo and behold on our plates were thick tender steaks and as many vegetables as we could wish for. Tante Go it would appear had a contact in the local black market to be able to produce this kind of food. Needless to say, we tucked in ravenously listening to the French conversation of the others around the table. Dédée mentioned that there would be six other 'parcels' on the train to St Jean de Luz, and this was the first time I had heard the term. It was certainly an apt word for this incredible delivery organisation to use.

It turned up once again when we were making ready to leave after lunch. Tante Go produced a book in which were recorded all the servicemen 'parcels' who had passed into Spain ahead of us. Offering me a pen she invited me to write my name under the last one recorded. 'You are parcel 82,' she said, laughingly.

As I wrote my full name I ran my eyes over the names ahead of me and picked out Jack Newton, a gunner friend from 12 Squadron, and two other members of my squadron, Flight Lieutenant L.C. Pipkin and Gordon Mellor, both navigators, and now most probably back in England. This gave me a tremendous boost of confidence and I passed the book to Smitty with a cry of delight.

Dédée decided meanwhile that my overcoat would be an

unnecessary burden so this was exchanged for a short-sleeved woolly jumper, which together with my suit, thick shirt and aircrew silk vest and long johns would stand me in better stead for the mountain part of the journey. Smitty's thicker suit was sufficient to withstand the cold, without any further reinforcement.

Tante Go handed us our local permits and we said goodbye to her and Bobonne as we slipped out the back of the villa into a quiet lane, Dédée walking with Smitty and B. and I bringing up the rear. One or two people were about as we made our way to the station, occasionally giving us a second glance as if to verify that we were strangers to the area.

As before, entry to the station platform caused no problem and we stood against a shelter wall until a shabby old train came in pulling old fashioned carriages made up of individual compartments with plain wooden six-a-side seats. An empty compartment stopped opposite me and I grabbed a window seat on the side nearest the sea and the other three took their separate corners. The sea views on the way to St Jean de Luz were breathtaking with the mysterious rising hills ahead, seemingly an impenetrable barrier. It was becoming increasingly hard to remain cool calm and collected and I was bursting with impatience as we steamed into the station of St Jean de Luz.

These feelings all disappeared when I observed that there were two policemen at the barrier. Maybe this was going to be the last hurdle so far as paper checks were concerned and nagging doubts took the place of impatience. We dropped onto the platform and moved to the exit, in my own case growing decidedly damp with perspiration. One by one we went through the barrier and praise be the permits and papers stood up to the test without need for questions.

Outside the station Dédée was standing indicating that we should move to the right, and there against the station wall was a selection of bicycles. Whilst Smitty and I were selecting our machines we were joined by none other than André and Marc from Madame Verdain's group, with three of their friends, Jacques, Nicholas and Poullen, and lastly Monsieur le Docteur from Brussels. Dédée quickly stopped any chit-chat and told us to move off at once down the road from the station.

I was already mounted, so, eager to be away, I started off at a fair clip with the others falling in behind, only to find Dédée pedalling furiously beside me and telling me to get over to the right-hand side.

In my excitement to get under way I had completely forgotten that the French drive on the right hand side of the road. On such silly mistakes the freedom of all could have been jeopardised, and it brought home to me the slender thread on which our helpers' lives rested. Suitably chastened I dropped back into the pack and we cycled on through the built-up area, into the countryside with the road becoming more and more uphill as we approached the foot of the mountains.

Outside the village of Urrugne Dédée called us to a halt and we left the cycles against a low wall. From there we were moving ever onward up and up on an unmade cart track feeling the muscles in the backs of the legs tightening under the unaccustomed exercise. The long days of sitting around doing nothing had softened our bodies and I was beginning to understand why Dédée and her helpers were so concerned about our fitness. Monsieur le Docteur was starting to breathe quite heavily and I had some doubts whether he would make it.

Release was at hand though, because we were led into the entrance to a farm and I remembered from Tante Go's briefing that we would be waiting here for a guide. I was ready for a rest and it was paradise as we were welcomed inside the farmhouse into a large room with a roaring fire and chairs a plenty! We sank down amid sighs of relief and took our footgear off. Here we met Francia, the farmer's wife, a gentle soul with an oval Madonna-like face. Her children moved around, stopping at each one of us and staring into our faces with soft brown eyes. Francia rebuked them in her soft Basque tongue and hustled them away to an inner room before she busied herself handing out bowls of hot milk and bread.

Dédée called to us to gather round the table in the room and explained in English and French that we would be starting off at night fall and that we would be walking with little rest for maybe twelve hours. To cross the border between France and Spain, we would need to ford the Bidassoa, a river at that time of the year swollen with additional rain water and very turbulent, but it was passable with the expert guidance of the man we were waiting for who would be known to us as Florentino, a Basque, who knew the mountains like the back of his hand. There was to be no smoking, no talking, no coughing, no lagging behind and any orders given must be obeyed without question, even if it meant lying face down in snow or mud or whatever. Dédée asked Monsieur le Docteur whether he wanted to change his mind in view of the strenuous walk ahead, but he smiled bravely and said he would keep up with the youngsters.

We broke up for the while and sat in small groups chatting in front of the fire. André and the lads explained that they had been sheltered by other families in Belgium and had been brought to Bayonne and St Jean de Luz separately by other Comète helpers. They were over the moon to have the chance to join our party; the other young Frenchmen would have to wait their turn in houses round about the Bayonne area, under the supervision of Tante Go.

The chattering ceased on the arrival of a huge man dressed in a dark blue smock and heavy dark linen trousers, traditionally worn by the local fishermen. His long craggy face, weather-beaten and walnut-coloured, had a kind of rugged nobility and was topped with a flat black beret. This then was Florentino and the more we came to know him we marvelled at his strength, his ability to sense danger and his instinctive feel for the mountains which enabled him to cover ground in pitch darkness at a tremendous pace avoiding obstacles and finding safe places to rest. We had cause to be thankful for his kindness and patience as he shepherded us into safety.

Around his neck Florentino was carrying several pairs of roped soled shoes or espadrilles, and a collection of goatskin bottles or *botas*. He unloaded this lot onto the table and had a long conversation with Francia, who relayed some part of it to Dédée. Apparently he spoke only Basque but had learnt one or two phrases in French and Spanish to assist him in his duties as a guide. Every now and then he would take a pull at his own *bota*, filled with his favourite cognac which he used much as an engine uses fuel. We were fascinated by his studied carefulness as he prepared us for the crossing.

One by one we sat before him to be fitted with our espadrilles which would enable us to move silently and keep footholds on poor surfaces. Florentino took some time with each, and in the case of Monsieur le Docteur examined his bare feet and applied bandages on those parts which would cause the most trouble. It hadn't occurred to me till then that anyone contracting blisters could jeopardise the safety of the whole party by slowing up its progress. Dédée then checked everyone's clothing and told me to turn my jacket and trousers inside out. Now I realised why that atrocious black lining had been provided. When I had finished reversing the suit I could see that with a black beret I was going to be virtually invisible even with a light shining on me, provided of course that the background was darkish.

With everybody clothed for the journey as best as could be

provided it was time for a farewell meal, and Francia and a young girl helper brought in soup stiffened with chunks of meat, and some delicious farmhouse bread. Nervous anticipation had somehow given everyone an appetite and there was little left for the friendly farm dogs. There was no time for leisurely digestion.

Florentino and Dédée cleared a place on the table and laid a large scale map before us. Quickly they ran over the landmarks which would help us to check our progress. From the top of the mountains immediately before us we should see the beam of the lighthouse at Fuenterrabia and the lights of the buildings in Irun, then we would descend to the river Bidassoa. Once across that and the road to Irun we would be in Spain with a great deal of walking yet to do, to reach a farmhouse well inside the frontier. On our left in the final stages we should see the unmistakable shape of the mountain known as the Three Crowns. Nodding to signify that we had absorbed the information we made ready to leave, Florentino gravely handing us a *bota* and a stout stick each.

# CHAPTER TEN

# The Crossing

Francia and B. stood at the farmhouse door shaking hands with each member of the party as they went out.

'See you in Piccadilly, old boy,' said B. gaily, as if we were out for a hike. Francia looked into my eyes, as her children had done, and I returned her smile warmly.

Outside Dédée was marshalling the party, having also changed into a dark blue smock and trousers. Florentino would of course, lead, then the five French lads, followed by Smitty, myself and Monsieur le Docteur and Dédée. Both Florentino and Dédée carried rucksacks containing odd items of food, and clothing either for us or themselves. Darkness was falling quite quickly and some light rain dampened our faces but not our spirits. What lay ahead was an adventure in itself, but what better support could you have than this pair of indomitable characters, the giant Basque powerful and resolute and the young resourceful slip of a girl who had made this organisation possible.

We formed up in a single file facing uphill. Florentino took a long swig out of his *bota* and waved us forward. The long and arduous upward climb had begun. At first the ground was covered in short tufted grass and was kind to the feet, but it wasn't long before we were on a stony slippery path helping ourselves along with our thick sticks. The early stars were beginning to twinkle and the air was growing decidedly cooler but the rain had stopped and we were climbing at a steady rate.

I could hear Monsieur le Docteur immediately behind me which heartened me somewhat and I prayed that he would be given superhuman strength for the journey. At least he was breathing regularly without gasps; the cold air would not cause him too much trouble if he kept his mouth shut. A loose stone caused me to stumble and fall on one knee and I realised that I was better occupied in making sure that I kept out of trouble rather than concerning myself with the other 'parcels', whose safekeeping was in much more capable hands. As if to confirm my thoughts Dédée moved past me going forward to check that everyone was feeling comfortable with the pace.

Although the outline of Smitty's back was beginning to be difficult to discern in the dark, up ahead against a backdrop of bright stars I could pick out the distant crests of the upper mountains. It seemed a hell of a long way to the top and all I could do was bend forward against the slope and feel my toes taking the strain. Occasionally an overhanging part of a shrub or plant of some sort would slap across my face having been disturbed by Smitty ahead of me. Dédée went back down the line to her allotted place at the rear giving Monsieur le Docteur an encouraging pat on his shoulder. The ascent became even steeper and the stout sticks were proving to be a godsend although they were giving out an audible click as they were pressed into the stony soil.

Without a word the message was passed down the line to stop, each person putting his hand back to stop the next one behind him. Florentino and Dédée exchanged quick whispers after which she grouped us in a semi circle.

'We are entering the area patrolled by French police and the military. Make as little noise as possible,' her voice was just audible.

Any idea that we were about to have a rest was soon put out of our heads. Off we went again but much more carefully which slowed progress down a little, although we were helped for some distance by reaching a plateau where the going was easier and the calf muscles regained a little relaxation from the incessant pushing up the slopes. Nothing lasts for long however in that part of the country and before long we were pressing upwards again.

Both Smitty and Monsieur le Docteur fell flat at this point, more out of awkwardness than fatigue. We got them to their feet quickly and then had to race forward to catch up with the others. Twice Florentino halted the column and we stood like stags trying unsuccessfully to pick out of the silence and darkness what it was that had alerted him. Satisfied of our safety he motioned us on with just a soft '*Tais-toi*', (or 'quiet'), coming from his lips.

The crest ahead drew rapidly nearer, producing a little more enthusiasm in tired limbs. As we reached the top the awful realisation came upon me that I could make out a further crest in the distance and even a series of crests beyond that. We had by no means finished the climb and I was willing Florentino to call a brief halt. As if by magic we heard him hiss a word and Dédée from the back loudly whispered, 'Down!' We fell to the ground, faces touching cold stones. Not before time, as it happened. Lying there in silence I could hear faint voices carried by the cold clear air, making my heart beat rapidly with the anticipation of being discovered. Minutes went by with the coldness rising from the ground penetrating the thickest clothes. The danger must have passed though because suddenly Florentino was on his feet beckoning us on. Obviously this was no place to stay for Florentino set off at a much faster pace moving in a zigzag fashion more to counter the gradient than to throw any pursuing quarry off course. The upper air was getting very cold and crisp and I climbed robot like watching my breath condensing in staccato gasps.

We had one more emergency stop dropping on one knee and waiting, waiting, waiting, for Florentino to return. He came back carrying another *bota* and a spare set of espadrilles and had another long pull of whatever the *bota* contained before starting off again. We were still under orders not to touch our own *botas* until we had been given permission, making it very hard for us watching Florentino sampling his, but we knew of his belief that it helped to sharpen his senses, and we were prepared to let him have it all if necessary.

The climb was on once more but the next crest came much sooner than I expected. True there looked to be more ahead but much closer than before, indicating that we were reaching the point where we would descend for the first time. Seawards an intermittent flash lit the far sky, not near enough to illumine our path but enough to suggest that we were not far from sighting the lighthouse on the Spanish part of the coast. Florentino was striding out now and not pausing to check any suspicious occurrence; clearly we were in a safe area where patrols didn't operate. Despite the fact that my leg muscles were aching the rest of the climb to the top became easier as my spirits rose. Behind me Dédée had been a constant source of support for Monsieur le Docteur who had done really well to stay the pace, knowing that this initial climb was the hardest physical test we would have on the journey.

Wisps of cloud began to cover the stars as we struggled on and we met up with a thin powdering of snow which covered the ground until the final crest where it disappeared, magically it seemed, but only because light rain had fallen there. In the shadow of some boulders we finally stopped for a short rest. Bread and cheese appeared from the rucksacks borne by Florentino and Dédée and he passed round his large *bota*, Dédée making sure that we did not take

**Above Left** The de Greef family in 1943, taken by a Biarritz photographer. Standing: Fernand (l'Oncle), Frederic. Sitting: Elvire (Tante Go), Bobonne (Elvire's mother), Janine and Dickie the beagle (*Janine de Greef via A.W. Cooper*).

**Above Right** Elvire de Greef.

**Below** The Bidassoa river.

**Above** January 1945 at Istres near Marseille after the invasion of the South of France. I am fourth from the left.

**Below** Myself (left) and a friend, Eddie Cardoza, in June 1946 after demobilisation.

too much! She was also concerned that while we rested we massaged the overworked calf muscles which had got us this far. Since it was harder to massage one's own legs we paired off and I had the benefit of Monsieur le Docteur's professional skills. Neither Dédée nor Florentino, of course, needed such pampering.

We were almost like new men as we rose for the next stage, making light work of the remaining hundred yards to the top of the world, or so it seemed. A fantastic sight awaited us, all Spain lay before our eyes, the myriads of twinkling lights in the town of Irun, the lighthouse at Fuenterabbia and farther in the distance the glow from San Sebastian. More used to living in blacked-out England, it reminded me of what lay ahead when peace was won and we could have as many lights burning as we wished. The sky had thickened up although no more rain was falling and immediately below the dark side of the mountains fell away to meet at their base the river which was not visible, except the short stretch lit by Irun down to our right. Florentino checked our espadrilles once more, Dédée satisfied herself that her 'parcels' were in order, gave the command once again that there must be no noise, and the descent began without our sticks which we left behind.

Anyone who thinks that after a long climb going down is much easier, should have their legs tested. For the first few hundred yards I experienced with some surprise more pain in my calf muscles than at any time previously. The descent was necessarily jerky with the weight of my body hitting my feet at every step. Despite the call for complete silence whispered oaths around me confirmed that others were having the same trouble. There were also more rocks and large stones on this side of the mountains inflicting painful bumps on the careless or unsighted. Once again Florentino began his zigzag manoeuvre and at about this time the ground grew softer and large bushes and small trees made their appearance. We stopped maybe three times while Florentino listened for trouble, but each time after a period of hair raising suspense, we heard his hoarse '*Doucement, doucement*' and moved on downward once more. Presumably this side of the mountains was as stiff with patrols, if not more so. Florentino was certainly showing more concern.

Vegetation grew thicker and it was almost impossible to move silently with low leaves and plants flapping against fast moving feet. There were more trees too and in the background we began to hear the growing rumble of the river down below. It sounded like a distant torrent or weir and the thought of entering that did not appeal to me one bit. Up above the clouds had cleared although more and more of the sky was being obscured by the upper branches of trees. At that point I felt that we must be safely hidden from view, fortunately so, because with the increasing darkness brought about by the thicker cover of trees we were blundering into each other much more often.

Florentino brought the column to a halt on a small plateau and he and Dédée went over to a gap in the trees to take a look through a fringe of high bushes. Dédée waved us over and we looked down on a fast flowing foaming river giving off a low roar as it pushed its way to the sea. To our left on the opposite bank there was a building of sorts lit up quite brightly with dark figures moving about.

'The Spanish Frontier post', Dédée explained. 'Now we go down to the river.'

The last part of the descent had to be effected by holding on to any part of the clothing of the person immediately ahead which came to hand. This was no time to lose contact with the group and visibility was extremely poor as we encountered more and more low hanging branches. The noise of the rushing water was drowning any that we were making, and it was a great relief to finally break through the trees to congregate by the river bank.

We turned our backs on the river to make ourselves less visible whilst Dédée explained how we would cross. Trousers would be removed and the legs tied in a knot behind our necks. The loose ends of the trousers would serve as a handhold for the person behind enabling the column to enter the water as a connected whole. Occasionally a small searchlight operated by the frontier guards was shone down river to detect smugglers crossing the water. If and when the command was given we must stop and bend as low as we could against the water but under no circumstances were we to look towards the light.

We nodded that we understood and began to divest ourselves of our trousers. Dédée gave a gasp of horror as I revealed my white silk long johns and told me in no uncertain terms to take them off with my trousers and to tie both garments around my neck. It would not matter in the water but emerging on the other side of the river I would be presenting a very white target for any guard on the alert. Duly chastened I did as I was told, feeling the cold air around my naked legs, and elsewhere. Florentino, meanwhile, had been tying a length of rope around the base of one of the riverside trees, satisfying himself that it would hold his weight. Dropping the rope he came over to check our espadrilles once more, there was no end to his concern for the safety of the party and he was obviously not going to risk someone losing his footing over a badly tied espadrille. Several of us were beginning to shiver, not only from the cold. Monsieur le Docteur looked all in, his large eyes shining out of a haggard face. He steadied himself by holding my upper arm and together we watched Florentino descend into the swirling water.

The giant Basque pushed himself into the fast moving current to the extent of his rope and then turned to face us, holding the rope taut. He nodded his head and we quickly formed into the same column as before.

'Take the rope,' hissed Dédée. '*En avant.*'

One by one we entered the water holding on to the rope for dear life. Florentino was well up to his waist and I wondered what the greatest depth of water was going to be. The water was icy cold and already the current was pushing against my legs making moving forward a slow process. By the time the column had reached Florentino the water was up to my chest and I was fighting to keep my balance. Florentino turned round and André linked up with him as we each took hold of the trouser legs around the neck of the man ahead of us. I felt the hard grip of Monsieur le Docteur behind me, and prayed once more that he would make it.

We began to move forward slowly again, Florentino had let go of the rope and we were at the mercy of the river as the column swayed to and fro in the rushing torrent. Lights were flashing about ahead and I suddenly realised that these were coming from vehicles going to and from Irun. The whole business seemed terribly unreal, but there was little time to dwell on one's situation as total concentration was necessary to fight off the pull of the river.

We seemed to be more than half way over when we came to a halt, and the word was passed back to get down against the water. Keeping my head low and looking downstream I could see the trees on the opposite bank palely illuminated and the light slowly moving towards the bank we had left. A short pause and we were upright again continuing our battle with the river. The searchlight sweep must have been a token affair because there were no more incidents and such danger as was present was coming from the current which grew even stronger as we drew nearer the opposite bank.

Then, as if by the hand of Providence, the pressure disappeared and we waded forward into calmer shallows, eventually to throw ourselves flat on a soggy meadow bordering the river bank. Florentino banged us all on the back and moved quickly to the cover of some low growing trees where we sank exhausted not caring for a moment about the lack of clothing around our legs. We soon began to shiver and Dédée crawled amongst us quietly insisting that we must massage our legs to get the circulation moving and to get our trousers back on as soon as possible. The next few minutes were spent regaining our composure as we hurriedly kneaded our leg muscles.

Surprisingly my trousers and long johns were reasonably dry and I managed to haul and tug them over my damp legs helped by the fact that time was of the essence and that although we had managed to cross the river we were still in a pretty vulnerable and desperate position. Florentino and Dédée lay close together for a while discussing their next move after which Florentino went off into the darkness. He returned very quickly and Dédée gathered us together.

'We have to climb up to the railway, cross it and climb again to the side of the road to Irun,' she whispered. 'When you are there Florentino will send you across the road one by one. When he signals you to go, run quickly and do not stop.' Her pale face seemed to shine in the darkness, her eyes serious and determined. 'Do you understand?' she asked. We nodded again. 'Good. *En avant!* Let's go.'

Florentino struck off and we formed in our customary line behind him making audible sucking noises with our feet as we pulled them out of the swamp-like meadow. We halted and Florentino's hoarse whisper of '*Doucement, doucement*' came clearly back to us. We took a little longer after that to make each step but the noise was cut down appreciably and we lumbered to the foot of the slope without further admonition. Florentino went up the slope like a monkey picking out handholds and roots to assist him even though there was little light. We made hard work of it behind him but found enough undergrowth to heave ourselves to the top. Dédée had a tougher job shoving Monsieur le Docteur from behind; he hadn't yet got over his river crossing which had taxed him both physically and mentally. The younger men were not much better and it came as a considerable shock to realise how tough this slip of a girl was, able not only to look after herself but also to virtually carry a 'passenger' in this manner.

Scrambling to the top we found ourselves on a railroad track curving away to our left around the bend of the river. The curve of the railway was faintly lit by the lamps outside the frontier post. Florentino was already on the other side of the track frantically waving us on. Smitty and I gave a final helping hand to Dédée and

Monsieur le Docteur who had almost completed the first climb, and we four joined the others jumping across the iron rails like gazelles.

The next climb to the road to Irun was much easier to accomplish because of the thicker growth of the bushes and softer soil under foot. Hauling ourselves up with branches we made quick work of the slope to find Florentino lying prone in a flat area behind the trees fringing the road. Once again he waved, this time to lie down and we bunched up together just behind him. He was studying the frontier post away to the left, hardly acknowledging Dédée as she crawled up beside him. They spoke in a low monotone after which Dédée clapped him on the back as if in accord.

She wriggled over to us to whisper that the order of crossing the road would be the two RAF first, then Monsieur le Docteur, then the five French lads. Obviously the risk of discovery would be greater each time someone made a run across the road which was reasonably well lit, and it was the object of the organisation to give priority to the return of Allied airmen.

Dédée tapped Smitty's shoulder and said, 'You first. Over the road, up the hill opposite and keep climbing until you see a large rock. Get behind it and wait.'

He looked back at me for a moment and then went forward beside Florentino. Time passed while we lay prone as two cars roared by on their way to the coast, and then Smitty rose up in a crouch. Florentino had his hand up like a parachutist dispatcher. Down it dropped and Smitty was away and running over to the other side and up the hill opposite gradually disappearing in the darkness beyond the road lights. I moved up beside Florentino with my heart thumping.

Out of the side of my eye I could see Florentino observing the movement of the sentries further up the road. He waited a few moments then he raised his arm in the air and I went down in the runner's crouch poised to make the fastest dash of my life. Down came his arm and I was away in a controlled panic reaching the other side of the road in seconds. There was a narrow verge and the hill-side began immediately. I hardly sensed the difference in levels as I was running in an 'every man for himself' situation and never slackened my pace.

Having passed through the lit area my eyes were once again getting used to the darkness and I could see the far hump of the top of the hill against the cloudy sky. But where, oh where, was the big rock? Had I missed it? I must have had several seconds of anxiety

before I picked out a dull shape ahead and to my right. It was a large
rock all right and I ran over to it and held on catching my breath.
Lurching round the back I discovered the prone figure of Smitty.
Dropping down beside him I patted his chest and we both shook
hands and laughed.

'We made it,' I gasped thankfully.

'So far,' countered Smitty. 'Welcome to Spain anyway.'

We strained our ears for sounds of the next runner becoming a
little anxious at the growing interval of time since I had arrived.
Then over the cold night air came rustling sounds making us sit up in
alarm because it seemed that more than a single person was coming.
Two figures came around the rock providing me with instant goose
pimples. One was panting heavily and I quickly perceived it was
Monsieur le Docteur and that Dédée had elected to run with him. He
collapsed beside Smitty whilst she slipped off her rucksack.

She came over to us smiling, saying, 'So. We have done the hard
bit. When the others get here we will have a short rest and a bite of
something to eat. Then we have several hours' more walking to do,
but the terrain is much better and there is far less danger.'

One by one the French lads turned up which called for a round of
congratulations each time, and lastly, after a longer wait, Florentino
himself unruffled and breathing easily. He slipped off his rucksack
and had another long draught from his *bota*, before finding Dédée for
a short parley. More cheese and bread came from the rucksacks
together with permission from Dédée to drink from our own *botas*.
However we could only have a mouthful or two, there was a long
journey ahead yet. The small *botas* contained a harsh brandy, heady
enough in normal circumstances but in our elated condition liable to
produce intoxication very quickly. We lay quietly eating and taking
occasional sips, slipping gently into a state of complete contentment
in the knowledge that we had stolen out of Occupied Europe under
the expert guidance of these two legendary persons.

Florentino made one more inspection of our espadrilles and
donned his large rucksack. It was time to go. Monsieur le Docteur
had recovered his composure even to wearing a wan smile. We
patted his shoulder encouragingly as we got back into our line,
hearing Florentino's '*Doucement, doucement*' even before we started.
Pushing up the first hill we found that Dédée's description of the
terrain was spot on, as one would expect. The slopes were more
gentle and the ground firm yet springy under the feet. Hearts filled
with joy we raised our eyes to the peaks ahead, striding out manfully.

Much as we encountered on our first climb from the farmhouse the hills rose to mountains in undulating waves and each succeeding crest gave rise to more beyond. Our euphoria gained from our *botas* lasted maybe an hour, after which we were back to the prolonged calf strain, albeit the slopes were more gentle.

At the top of one rise we had a glimpse of the brightly lit town of San Sebastian further along the coast, and it would have been great to have begun a descent then and there. But our route was further inland giving us several hours of mountain walking to complete. Florentino stopped the column after a few hours, for a brief rest under some overhanging rock. One of the French lads had sore feet requiring bandaging which gave us an opportunity to take the weight off our feet.

As a special treat Florentino handed round his large *bota* containing a raw red wine, an honour in one sense and a miracle in the other that he hadn't drank it all! Whatever else, the rest did us good breaking up the monotony of the endless waves of land.

Shortly after leaving our resting place it was noticeable that we were on much more level ground, light was beginning to show in the sky allowing us to see greater distances. Dédée called out from the back to look over to the left and there in the background was the huge bulk of the Peña de Aya the mountain with three peaks, known as the 'Three Crowns'. It stayed there hardly moving as we walked on and on seemingly on a merry go round. Florentino kept looking back and egging the flagging party on with his phrase '*Dos cien metros*'. Just another two hundred metres more; some joke, but it did serve to keep us moving forward. Dédée also chipped in with a few exhortations and this was more fruitful since we weren't going to show ourselves any more weary than she.

It was very heartening when we hit a well used mountain track and began to veer towards the Three Crowns. Although it took a while the distance between us and the mountain was eaten up and we passed fairly close to it but having to traverse rising ground at the same time. Climbing again started up the old calf muscle fatigue, which added to the general fatigue which hung heavily over us and I pressed forward painfully hoping that this part of the walk would be short. Struggling to the top of the rise we were rewarded with a panoramic view of the lights of the coast and the little villages in the low lying areas down below. Without stopping we began to come down from the mountains in semi darkness leaving the barer ground for more gentle slopes where sheep had been grazing. The undulating waves of land were now going downwards lifting our morale appreciably. The slopes gave way to fields and cart tracks reaching down into the valleys at the foot of the hills.

Dawn came quickly as we descended, and coming out of a large meadow we were confronted by a low lying farmhouse. Florentino went forward to the building where after a few moments a light flicked on and a female form stood framed in the doorway. He waved us to come onward which we did with surprising alacrity. Within seconds we were being welcomed into a large room with a long table already set out as if for a restaurant meal. The Comète organisation left nothing to chance.

The farmer's wife bustled about the room, stoking the fire and taking from us damp clothing which could be drying whilst we were eating. As for us, we just took a chair each at the table and waited until this ample vigorous lady could bring us something to eat and drink. We were extremely hungry and very tired and one or two heads were dropping forward onto the white tablecloth. Incredibly Monsieur le Docteur was just lounging back with his eyes closed, a beaming smile dividing his face in two. His, above all, was the greatest achievement. Smitty and I solemnly toasted him in water before falling upon the huge omelettes that began to arrive. It was indeed a memorable breakfast, the chatter and laughter was unnaturally depressed as a safety precaution to protect our Spanish hosts but we managed a quiet celebration nevertheless.

Whilst we were sitting about waiting for our clothes to dry, Florentino and Dédée went off to change into the clothes they had brought with them and reappeared in much the same gear but completely dry. Dédée singled out Smitty and me and told us to get dressed as we were to be picked up by car within the hour. I asked about the others, to be informed that they would be making their own arrangements. Smitty and I spent the rest of the time exchanging names and addresses and generally saying goodbye to each of our companions on the perilous journey we had undertaken. We had become a family by that time united by the same kind of bond which exposure to danger imposes on any fighting group, and naturally vowed that we would all meet again after the war.

Dédée eventually called for Smitty and me and, after solemnly shaking hands with our good Spanish lady, we followed Dédée outside up a long farm track to a metalled road where a car was waiting. Florentino was leaning over a fence still checking for possible trouble and we went over to shake his hand and kiss him on both cheeks, making him smile and nod his head gravely.

A young man standing by the car came forward to greet us in polished English and it was then I noticed the CD plates on the car. He opened the car door and motioned for us to enter, but before doing so we turned to say our farewell to Dédée.

Her eyes were twinkling as she said, 'Goodbye, you two. It wasn't so bad, was it?'

I shook my head saying, 'No. Bless you for all you have done for us and the guidance of Florentino. I shall remember you always.' As an afterthought I added, 'Are you staying at the farm long?'

She gave a broad smile. 'No, no, no. We go back tonight.'

To say that I was amazed would be a complete understatement. To think that a long arduous journey which had knocked the stuffing out of more than a half a dozen strong young men could be undertaken in reverse after a rest of a few hours, was beyond my imagination. And yet these two differing in many ways, but equal in bravery and daring would be doing so again and again, the tall agile Basque and this young Belgian girl, who between them had the strength of many. I just shook my head, kissed her hand and got inside the car. Smitty had a further word and went so far as a hug. Her face uptilted was visible from the back window for some time as she waved us off.

# CHAPTER ELEVEN

# Under the Flag

We stayed looking out of the back window until the figure in the distance grew too small to be recognised. Settling back against the leather seats we stared out of the side windows of the car, hardly taking in the passing scenery, our minds racing over the events of the last day. Our ruminations were broken by the measured tone of the driver:

'Feeling a bit tired? Don't worry, we're on our way to the Consulate in San Sebastian. You'll get a bit of a rest there before we move you on to Madrid. By the way, when we stop outside the Consulate I want you to dart inside as quickly as you can. We don't want to advertise what we are doing. The Spaniards might take umbrage.'

His friendly manner prompted us to ask a few questions about the route to England but to all of them he replied, 'Later on, old chap.'

We got the message and bothered him no more, taking growing notice of the sights as we went along. The coast came into view with the sea glistening in pale sunlight. Peasants were making their way to market filling the road with a miscellany of vehicles. Our driver threaded through them with ease, some falling back in deference as they observed the flag on the bonnet. I felt very grand and catching Smitty's eye I waved my hand in royal fashion to the people outside. He followed suit bringing a fast rebuke from our driver who had just observed us in his rear mirror:

'I realise you are feeling a little happy and high spirited, but whilst you are travelling under our care you must at no time attract attention to yourselves. Understand?' We nodded in unison returning to our window-watching, fascinated by the different styles of building and the bright colours in which they were painted.

Before long we were in the outskirts of San Sebastian, clean and white against the blue sky, and here we branched off towards the sea. Around a bend stretched a long promenade filled with strollers taking advantage of a fine winter's day.

Our car slowed down and our driver addressed us once more. 'As soon as I stop and get out, move towards the door I'm heading for. I will open it and you will enter not looking in either direction.' The authority in his voice brooked no argument or question.

If we were expecting to draw up before an imposing edifice we were greatly disappointed. The car stopped at one of a row of flat fronted undistinguished buildings. Smitty and I followed our driver through the door, as directed, straight onto a staircase which we mounted at speed. Passing through an enquiry room we were ushered into the presence of the Deputy Consul, a tall dapper man who came forward in greeting.

'Glad to have you here, gentlemen. No doubt you are pretty tired from your travels. May I suggest you first make use of the bathroom facilities and give my colleague here an idea of what clean clothing you require. Your outer garments will be cleaned up as far as possible and returned to you before you leave. Arrangements have been made for you to travel to Madrid after lunch, by car of course, as previously. At least you will spend Christmas in reasonable surroundings.'

'Christmas Eve?' I said in amazement.

'Yes, it's the 24th December today, you know. Probably you've lost count of the days since you came down.' He seemed quite amused at our surprise. 'Anyway I'll see you again later on. Unfortunately the Consul is away at the moment. I know that he would have liked to have welcomed you himself. Have a good clean up!'

Another young consular official came over and shepherded us through another couple of doors to a rest room with two beds. 'The bathroom is next door,' said he in parting. 'Use the dressing gowns there and I'll come back to find out what underclothing you need.'

Smitty and I dropped onto the beds in joyous relief. 'Merry Christmas, goddammit,' he bellowed. 'Who's first in the bathroom?'

We had nothing in our pockets which we could use to toss with, so for a hilarious moment we scoured the room for something finally settling on one of the cups underneath the bed castors. Smitty won and disappeared, already practising a bathroom aria. I just lay and listened to his happy voice, reflecting on the unselfish sacrifices which people had made to get me there, and letting their faces float through my mind. I must confess that I found myself crying.

Smitty returned his face coloured pink and shiny, wearing a light blue dressing gown. 'All yours,' he beamed. 'Gee it's great!'

I needed no invitation and was soon deep in lather feeling all the tension flowing out of me. After shaving and cleaning my teeth with an actual toothbrush I was ready for the rest of the day. Back in the rest room we waited for our consular friend, flat out on the beds provided. He wasted no time for he was soon in to pick up our suits, carrying the shirts and underclothing, socks and sweaters we had ordered. We dressed as far as we could feeling completely clean for the first time for days. The Deputy Consul made his appearance taking brief particulars of our identity, when we had come down and how we had linked up with the Comète line. We would be fully debriefed elsewhere. He then advised us to get a few hours' rest, someone would call us for lunch and bring in the rest of our clothes including shoes, just prior to leaving.

Sleep came easily and it seemed only moments before we were being awakened. 'Sorry, chaps. Lunch in 15 minutes,' bellowed our consular friend.

We tumbled out of bed automatically as if we were on standby procedure. Hastily tidying ourselves and pulling our dressing gowns around us we followed him to a small room where a table had been laid out. We ate ravenously what was placed before us, to be honest I cannot remember what the meal comprised, but it was excellent and I had a cup of tea to follow, my first for months. Then back to the rest room where our suits had been laid out and a new pair of shoes neatly placed by each bed. Our original driver looked in to say that we would be leaving as soon as we were ready. We dressed in seconds and made our quick farewells to the staff in the outer rooms and lastly the Deputy Consul who once again reminded us to keep away from the car windows.

The same drill operated on the way out, the driver opened the street door and went towards the car with us following hot foot, looking straight ahead. We were in the car in virtually three seconds and off in five, giving no one a chance to register our departure. San Sebastian looked a busy town even in late December and passing pedestrians occasionally gave a quizzical look at the car's flag as it went by. The sights of the coast line were over all too quickly as we headed inland climbing through small villages and more often bare arid land. Surprisingly enough there was little traffic on the road and mostly we saw animal drawn carts, especially in the villages. As we went on the buildings in the villages grew more basic and the people moving about them were ill dressed and patently poor. It seemed such a stark contrast to the teeming prosperous coast. How the people lived in this barren environment was a mystery.

The monotony of the scenery was broken up a couple of times as we went first through Vitoria and then skirted Burgos, its walls looking quite striking in the afternoon sunlight, as the birthplace of El Cid should. But then we were back to rolling uplands climbing once more towards the high sierras. In a desolate spot we stopped for a few moments whilst the car took a rest and we took care of more pressing problems. The view, although stark, was truly majestic and the silence was eerie. One felt very close to nature or God, according to one's belief. The road was clear up there although there was plenty of snow in the higher mountains, somehow I didn't associate Spain with snow before then.

After a period of driving on this high plateau we descended once more to cross the river Duero with more high mountains ahead of us.

'That's the Sierra de Guadarama,' explained our driver. 'We'll stop up there for a bite to eat.'

We took some time to climb up to it with snow increasing on the slopes on either side of us, but the road appeared to have a charmed life and stayed dry.

Our driver hopped out and produced from the back of the car a wicker picnic box, suitably filled with sandwiches and such, even a bottle of white wine. We felt very civilised and genteel, learning once again how to take several bites at a sandwich rather than wolf away as we had begun to be accustomed. Our driver joined with us and we had a pleasurable half hour even though the air was thin and icy outside.

'It's downhill to Madrid now,' he said. 'When we get there it will be dark, but the city itself is attractively lit and you may be tempted to press your noses against the windows. Don't. Try to see as much as you can from a position away from them. It's really a lovely lively place.'

Thick cloud appeared as if from nowhere and a streak of lightning snaked across the high peaks like a whiplash. Rain followed and we moved off into instant mud but it didn't last, for as we descended the storm stayed behind and we finished the downhill leg into Madrid with the sky slowly filling with stars. Ahead was a blaze of light growing brighter with each mile, until the light was all around us and we were crossing a large road junction down a broad avenue lined with tall buildings. We had arrived in Madrid.

The street lighting and the illumination of the large buildings was overwhelming after having experienced the enforced darkness of London and other big cities. Smitty and I sat goggle-eyed at the kaleidoscope of magnificent squares, cobbled alleyways, narrow twisting streets, busy taverns and the impressive and lofty narrow arches through which the traffic passed at certain points. It was just too much, rather like looking at a superb cream cake through a baker's window. Abruptly, it was all over as we swept into the side entrance of the British Embassy a white building proudly displaying the Union flag. Our good friend, the driver, brought the car to a halt in the courtyard and came round to open the car door as if for the Ambassador himself. We got out onto British soil, and followed him to a long low building off the courtyard where he left us in the hands of the Embassy staff.

We were taken inside to a dormitory with several beds, some already occupied by previous Comète 'parcels', and others by young men whose reasons for being there we never investigated or referred to. Preparations were already afoot to celebrate Christmas Eve. After a preliminary round of introductions we were quickly absorbed into the party spirit and so began a memorable evening when all inhibitions disappeared and the joy of freedom lifted the heart. Some of the Embassy staff joined in, later to take part in some of the more hilarious games and stunts normally reserved for late nights in Bomber Command messes. In Smitty's language it was a hoot, and it was very late on Christmas morning when I surfaced in bed, still wearing the clothes I had arrived in.

By the time we were called to dinner in the adjacent dining room, we were all more or less tidied up and just as well because we received a visit from Sir Samuel and Lady Hoare, the Ambassador and his wife, to extend to us their Christmas greetings and the hope that we would soon be back with our families. They were a gracious couple and very keen to see that we had the best of care. Sir Samuel because of his responsibility towards Anglo-Spanish relations saw little of us, but Lady Hoare managed to allot some of her time to producing little jobs for us to do. Thus hardly a day passed without our idle hands being engaged in something useful.

Christmas Day passed quietly, most of us lounging and dreaming of home, culminating in the inevitable games of cards and a few 'nightcaps'. Rumour had it that a couple of the lads would be off soon to some unknown destination, they had been at Madrid a fortnight already. Smitty and I braced ourselves for a longer stay than we had envisaged. The rumour had not been unfounded because the day after Boxing Day, the two lads were called for and never returned. It was much like the ten green bottles but with a nicer overtone. Next day we had an interview with the Deputy Air Attaché who informed us that every effort was being made to clear all the existing 'lodgers' out to Gibraltar, and that we would be on the way in a week or two. Patience was the name of the game, meanwhile we were not in uncomfortable surroundings.

Apart from joining in the odd jobs produced by Lady Hoare we spent a lot of time keeping in trim with exercises, and I came across a Spanish grammar book which took up the rest of my attention during the remaining days at the Embassy. Each day saw another disappearance from the dormitory, balanced very rarely by a new arrival. Time came when we didn't need to be very astute to work out that our turn was imminent, confirmation of which reached us via the Deputy Air Attaché who late one evening informed Smitty and me that we would be leaving early the next morning for the consulate in Seville in company with Mac, one of the other 'lodgers'. The move to Seville instead of Gibraltar came as a surprise to us, but apparently this move had been successful on previous occasions and had provided a safer route to Gibraltar.

Dawn had not yet broken when we assembled in the courtyard to board an Embassy car, this time with a driver plus another official in the front passenger seat. There was no one about as we swept out of the Embassy entrance to cruise silently through a sleeping Madrid, passing the grand museums including the Prado, set back in its lovely tree lined avenue. What a pity that we couldn't take it all in, in daylight, but sightseeing was not the priority of our two guides, and we were soon gliding over a pretty bridge across the river Manzanares, and thereafter leaving the city suburbs at a steady rate of knots. The road was quite clear of traffic heading our way and much more level than the road in from the north. The sun came up pretty quickly as we reached the open dun coloured countryside, giving us after an hour or so a distant glimpse of Toledo up on its hill. There seemed to be greenery only in the river valleys, the rest was sunbaked and grim and the monotony of it gradually sent us to sleep, not unnaturally since we had risen early.

I awoke as a range of sierras loomed ahead to slowly pass by to our right. The stark beauty of the sierras outweighs the lack of plant life, but the peasant population must scratch out a very primitive life in the harsh conditions. Someone had told me once that Spain was a land of contrasts, perhaps I had come to that conclusion already, but we began to descend into a river valley fertile and warm, with lush growth all around, and it came to me how fortunate some people are to be born in the right places.

We passed through another small town and thereafter began to climb into higher land with a background of mountains which we would obviously be going through. The official sitting next to the driver slid back the interior window:

'That's the Sierra Moreno ahead. We'll be stopping for a breather and a bite at the top.'

We three 'parcels' discussed the peculiar habits of the diplomatic corps who preferred to eat in high places and came to the conclusion that we were less likely to meet any prying eyes up there. The stop did away with any sleepiness which we had. The air was very cold and knifed across the face razor sharp. After a brief run round the car and gasping at the distant view of the valley of the Guadalquivir at the end of which lay Seville, we elected to have our hot drink and sandwiches inside the car, in comfort. Our stay in Madrid had soon made us soft.

From then on we descended towards Seville with the countryside rapidly changing to prosperous little villages surrounded by orchards and groves of orange and lemon trees, something we had never seen before, vineyards and pretty little gardens, a veritable fairyland after the barren desolateness of the high plateaus and sierras. For some reason we bypassed Cordoba, probably it was either busy or dangerous, we never discovered, regaining the highway later for an hour long drive along the rest of the beautiful Guadalquivir valley. We were almost disappointed when the outskirts of Seville began to appear, but this was short lived as we entered this fantastic Moorish city, streets lined with orange trees and bursting with elegant buildings, exhibiting the Arabic influence in superb arches and fine tracery in stonework. At least we had the benefit of full daylight and the opportunity to see, if only for a brief moment, the Alcazar and the Cathedral.

A minute later and we were drawing up outside the British Consulate, a little more imposing than in San Sebastian. Our travelling official disappeared inside to emerge after some minutes to have words with our driver. We moved off away from the city centre and the interior window of the car slid back. 'It has been decided that you should stay away from the Consulate whilst you are waiting for the next stage of your journey. The Deputy Consul has kindly agreed to your staying with him for the while; we are on our way to his house now.'

The car pulled up in a bright little corner of Seville and under direction we disgorged swiftly from the car into a gleaming white villa, being greeted at the door by the Deputy Consul's wife, an attractive brunette who took us in to a large room which had been hurriedly converted into a small dormitory for us. She showed us where we could wash etcetera, and offered to have any laundry done quickly, pointing out on each bed, pyjamas, towel, soap, toothbrush and razor. She was kindness itself and had spent a lot of thought on our welfare.

Later on we were to meet her husband, an energetic, tall man with a grand sense of humour. It was he who briefed us on our final hurdle.

'What we are doing is getting you chaps out as members of the crew of British orange boats plying between Seville and Gibraltar. You will be here a night or two until the next boat arrives when we will make arrangements for your departure. Until then relax and let my wife know if you require anything.'

We got down to sleep that night in a high pitch of excitement, helped by liberal 'nightcaps' produced by our host and his wife. For the next couple of days we reverted to our exercise routine and reading, eating extremely well and rounding off each day with an evening's conviviality.

News of the arrival of an orange boat was brought to us by our host who returned from the Consulate on the third morning, with the additional and welcome information that the boat was due to turn round quickly and sail in two days. The next thirty-six hours were the hardest to bear of all; our host kept our morale going by making light of the inspection that we would have to endure by the Spanish police. When the captain of the vessel arrived with his mate at the villa in the late afternoon of sailing day, we were tense and eager to be off.

'We'll drive down to the entrance to the quay where we'll meet other members of the crew,' explained the captain, a stocky weather-beaten man. 'What I want you to do is to feign drunkenness so that you can be helped aboard between two genuine crew members. With luck the Spanish police will be lenient enough to wave you on.' The Deputy Consul laughed and said, 'There you are, I told you it would be simple.' It was then I had a brainwave. 'Perhaps it would help if we had a few drinks before we go, it would save us acting completely.' The Deputy Consul looked at the captain who nodded affably. 'Brilliant,' he roared. 'What's everybody having?'

After half an hour we three were ready for anything and we

boarded the captain's wagon in high spirits after a solemn farewell to
our hosts.

Approaching the quay side we stopped outside a small tavern
where a number of seamen had congregated. The captain and the
mate had a word with them and they began to file slowly over to the
boat, while three pairs broke off to join Smitty, Mac and I around a
couple of tables outside the tavern. For a few minutes we sat drinking
a raw red wine until a bell sounded on the boat.

'Here we go then, lads,' said the seaman next to me. 'You know
what you have to do. Give 'em a song or two.'

I cannot imagine what the sight of our progress looked to the
police waiting alongside the boat's gangway. Any fear I had was
completely dissolved and I sang my heart out in a drunken fashion as
I lurched between my good supporters. Smitty and Mac could be
heard in similar fashion but as we drew nearer to the boat we were
beginning to be drowned out by the stentorian tones of the captain
and his mate who were really giving us what for. The police were
actually laughing as we went past them rolling our eyes and
contorting our faces. Up the gangway being pushed from side to side
I was finally confronted by the Captain who cuffed my ear quite hard
and ordered me below. The two lads helping me steered towards a
hatchway and I made my way down below to a saloon cabin with
Smitty and Mac closely following.

We hardly had time to congratulate ourselves before the swarthy,
slim mate came below and ordered us to follow him. A succession of
doors, hatches, ladders and catwalks led us to a small confined space
somewhere in the bowels of the vessel. A square metal door in the
bulkhead was opened by the mate and we looked in.

'This is the propeller shaft locker,' he said. 'You'll be in here until
the boat is searched and we are out on the river on the way to the sea.
No one ever comes down here.' The propeller shaft seemed to take up
most of the room but we managed to squeeze in with our legs
underneath it, and with our chests some six inches away. 'See you in
a couple of hours,' said the mate cheerily and banged the metal door
shut. It was no time to develop claustrophobia. We sat in complete
darkness, oil and other nautical smells strong in our nostrils, not
daring to talk in case we revealed our presence.

After a lengthy interval all kinds of heavy knocking sounds
reverberated against the hull of the boat and to my horror the
propeller shaft began to revolve, faster and faster flashing past
within inches of my face. In the dark I heard a gasp of discomfort

from Smitty and a long drawn out 'Jee-susss' as he expelled his breath. The human mind and body being what it is, totally adaptable, soon came to our rescue and before long we were making joking remarks about the whining noise of the shaft, feeling able to raise our voices now that the boat was in motion. Our new found bonhomie had to stand the test of time because we must have had at least two hours in this noisy nautical dungeon, but I can remember leaning my head back against the bulkhead, smiling to myself in the dark and savouring the fact that we had made it.

How wrong I was! The metal door at last swung open to reveal the cheery countenance of the mate. 'Careful as you go, lads,' came his advice as we wriggled our cramped limbs out of the locker.

We stayed a moment or two massaging our leg muscles, and then followed the mate aloft to the saloon cabin where the Captain had a small celebration organised. Fortified by some excellent rum we learnt from him that we must stay below until the boat had cleared the river, after which we were welcome to join him and the mate on the bridge. 'We will be keeping close to the coast all the way to Gibraltar,' explained the Captain. 'Unfortunately there has been a deal of enemy submarine activity in the straits, one or two vessels have been lost on this run. Keep your fingers crossed, lads. You have been lucky so far.'

The feeling of uncertainty stayed with me for the rest of the voyage. When we eventually emerged in the evening light from down below the feel of wind against the face provoked instant thoughts of freedom, but the large number of lookouts confirmed that the race had not been run yet. There were anxious hours for us as we sailed in darkness past scenes of Britain's former glories, first Cadiz, then Cape Trafalgar, ending with our going below to snatch a few restless hours of sleep on the soft benches in the saloon cabin. There was nothing we could do as the boat slipped through the Straits of Gibraltar, except try to forget the ever present danger lurking beneath the surface. You can imagine our relief when we were woken to find the pale light of dawn filtering into the saloon cabin. Our friend the mate shouted to us to come on deck and we sleepily followed to stand at the bridge rail and see the imposing shape of the Rock of Gibraltar ahead.

Immediate joy and relief turned slowly to frustration as the hours went by with the Rock seemingly growing no bigger. The Captain noticed this, putting our minds at rest.

'Give it a couple of hours, lads. Go and have some breakfast.'

I noticed with trepidation on the way down to the dining saloon that the lookouts had been reinforced again. Despite this, breakfast was a hearty meal and we returned to our bridge station in better spirits although still half expecting to hear the thud and shudder of a torpedo.

It wasn't to be though, thankfully, and we sailed into Gibraltar harbour safe and sound. The myriads of war vessels made a marvellous and magnificent sight, backed by the massive shape of the Rock itself. As if in salute, an RAF Catalina flew low over our vessel and we waved at it like schoolboys. We stayed on the bridge mentally playing sailors until we had reached the orange boat wharf and the crew had secured their lines.

'Well lads,' said the Captain. 'I guess that's it. Glad to have had you aboard.'

We all shook his hand with a great deal of warmth. Since then the men of the Merchant Navy have had my total respect and admiration. The mate escorted us down to the gangway where we said our goodbyes to him and some of the men we had come to know in our short but perilous voyage. At the foot of the gangway stood two harbour policemen, to whom we made our way quite happily.

We stopped in front of them and one said, 'May I see your papers, gentlemen.' Amused, we answered that we hadn't any.

'Then I'm afraid you will have to be taken into custody.' We were astounded, until he smilingly added: 'There'll be some chaps along for you later.'

'Parcel 82' and two other 'parcels' had been safely delivered!

The story would not be complete without the reader knowing what became of all who are mentioned within it. To this end I have added a final chapter. . . .

# CHAPTER TWELVE

# The Cost

The return to England took place by sea, on a captured French liner built solely for the Mediterranean. It had a flattish bottom and the skeleton crew of Royal Navy men told us not to worry as any torpedo fired at us would pass underneath! We took our turns on watches, finding the heavy seas a trifle overwhelming both in the continual spray and in the exaggerated pitching of the vessel which returned quite a few meals to the deep. We docked at Gourock in Scotland on 26 January 1943.

After de-briefing in London and a couple of weeks' leave I reported back to RAF Uxbridge for re-posting. Since I was returning from the last operation of my second tour I was given the option to choose where I might be sent. Plumping for Ferry Command I returned home for two more days to await my posting. It came by telegram ordering me to report to RAF Lyneham, which I did to be

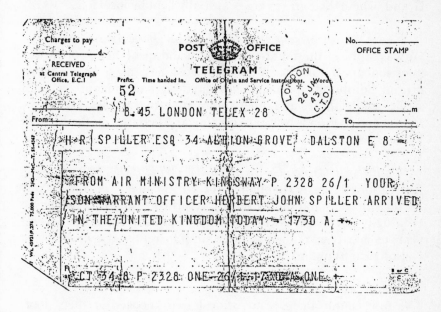

told that I was attached to a flight transporting VIP's to the Middle East. At that time Transport Command had not been formed. After a crash refresher course of astro-navigation, I was once again in the air en route to Cairo and landed in Gibraltar some five weeks after leaving it by ship, on the way to take part in the desert war. This fact, in itself, would have warmed the hearts of those gallant people who had done so much to return me, because they took great risks to get experienced aircrew immediately back into the war.

You may gather some idea about the risks involved, from the following accounts of some of the people in my story, based on such information as I have been able to obtain. I include among them the members of my crew: five of them gave their lives to save mine.

'Sid' – Squadron Leader Sidney Horace Fox, DFM (Pilot)
'Norman' – Flight Sergeant Norman Alexander Mercer (Rear Gunner)
'Phil' – Sergeant Philip Charles Heath (Mid-Upper Gunner)
'Fitz' – Sergeant Lawrence Fitzimmons (Flight Engineer)
Sergeant Henry Frederick Wood (Second Pilot)

All of the above were killed in action on the night of 24/25 October 1942, when the aircraft crashed near Ligny-en-Barrois, near Nancy. They are buried in a small village cemetery at nearby Nant-le-Grand, where their graves are beautifully kept by local folk.

*'Peewee' – Flight Sergeant Rowland Maddocks (Bomb Aimer)*
He was captured the day after baling out and spent the rest of the war in prisoner of war camps. A talented artist, he came back to set up a firm in Edinburgh specialising in the design and manufacturer of service and club ties and other commemorative articles. He is now retired and lives in a beautiful cottage at Aberlady, on the Firth of Forth.

*'Woolly' – Pilot Officer Geoffrey Wollerton (Wireless Operator)*
Also captured shortly after baling out. He remained a prisoner of war for the duration and on his release returned to the RAF which he eventually left in 1975 with the rank of squadron leader. Several years of charity work then followed until he retired. He now lives at Ketton near Stamford.

*Monsieur and Madame Lafrogne of Ligny-en-Barrois*
The first couple to help me after I had knocked at their door. Monsieur Lafrogne died of natural causes after the war but I am still

in touch with Madame Lafrogne who still has my flying suit and boot in her loft. Her children and grandchildren came and visited me a few years ago.

*'Antoine'– Antoine Renaud of Fourmies*
*'Edouard'– Edouard Verpraet of Fourmies*
Both the above were betrayed and arrested in April 1943. They were taken to Brussels and after several months suffering in prison, were executed by firing squad at the Tir National in Brussels on 20 October 1943, along with several other members of the Comète line. They are remembered in Fourmies by having streets named after them.

*'Judith'– Judith Renaud, Antoine's wife*
She survived interrogation and eventually died in 1980. She had many medals for her resistance activities and was given a civic funeral. I kept in contact with her until her death and still do with Fabien and Judith, her children. Agnès, a granddaughter, has also visited me.

*'Emmeline'– Emmeline Troclet, later Cézarine of Wignehies*
She married a resistance hero and after the war opened a hairdressing establishment. She is now a widow and retired but we still communicate regularly.

*Madame Bachelart of Momignies*
She lived until a few years ago, a farmer's widow of great strength and courage. Shortly after the war she had, to her own satisfaction, German prisoners of war working on her farm, under no illusions as to how much was expected from them.

*'Constance'– Elizabeth Liégeois of Brussels*
*'Nounou'– Elizabeth Warnon of Brussels*
Both these ladies were arrested and condemned to death by a Luftwaffe tribunal on 5 May 1943. They were deported to Germany to spend their days in various concentration camps, notably Ravensbrück and Mauthausen. Incredibly they survived and returned to Belgium to receive decorations from several countries. I have been to Belgium on one or two occasions to see them, probably the most notable was to take part with them at a function when the Queen and the Duke of Edinburgh made a state visit to Brussels. The

Grande Place was lined with members of the Belgian Resistance who were presented to Her Majesty and the Duke. Bursting with pride I stood between Constance and Nounou, as one of the invited party from the RAF Escaping Society. They are both happily still alive but need to spend some months each winter in the south of France for their health, which has never recovered from their days of dreadful privation.

### '*Aimable*' – *Aimable Fouquerel of Paris*

He worked as a masseur in a local hospital and put his flat at the disposal of the Comète organisation. Arrested in mid-1943, he was later executed by firing squad on 28 March 1944 at Mont-Valerien, Paris, together with Frédéric de Jongh, Dédée's father.

### *Dédée – Andrée de Jongh of Brussels*

The creator of the Comète organisation, daughter of Frédéric de Jongh who later took over the Paris section. She escorted well over a hundred airmen to safety, making the perilous double crossing of the Pyrenees 24 times. She was betrayed and arrested at the farmhouse in Urrugne on 15 January 1943, together with Francia, and ended up in Ravensbrück concentration camp. Her story is admirably told in the book *Little Cyclone* by Airey Neave. She was also lucky to survive and returned to Brussels later to receive among other decorations, the George Medal. She has since spent her life in charitable work at one time nursing lepers in Africa. A short while ago, very belatedly, she was made a Countess by the King of the Belgians.

### '*Tante-Go*' – *Madame Elvire de Greef of Anglet*

Although arrested at one time and released, she never gave up her work for Comète and stayed in her villa until the end of the war. She also received the George Medal. Happily she has survived and keeps close contact with the Royal Air Forces Escaping Society.

### '*Francia*' – *Francia Usandizanga of Urrugne*

Arrested with Dédée she was to die in the horror of Ravensbrück on the 12 April 1945, aged 36.

### '*Florentino*' – *Florentino Goicoechea of Ciboure*

He survived the war but not unscathed, being severely wounded in the leg in July 1944. He saw several hundred airmen over the dangerous route to Spain and he too was to receive the George

Medal, among other decorations. He died in July 1980, and is buried at the foot of his great love, the Pyrenees.

*'Monsieur le Docteur' – and the five French lads*
Were arrested by the Spanish police after leaving the farm on their way to San Sebastian. The last communication I received from them came from the Spanish concentration camp Miranda del Ebro, 40 miles south of Bilbao. They were hoping for a quick release.

Sadly I have never been able to contact Smitty or Mac or any of the people in St Dizier or Paris. There were many others, of course, who helped in my evasion and whom I never saw. The losses sustained by the members of the Comète organisation were considerable. Out of 800 helpers some 160 were executed or expired in the filthy, disease-ridden concentration camps, but the escape line never ceased, although at times it was a near thing. You can imagine then the sense of debt that hangs over me when I ponder on the fact that nine people died through helping me to live and return to duty. There are many who do not wish to be reminded of wars, and I respect their view because I want no more mass violence of that kind, but there is little enough recognition of the kindness and courage which stems from the ordinary people under war conditions. My story is of them, written in thanksgiving and tender memory.

# Index